Button Training for Dogs

Teach Your Dog to Talk: A Practical Guide to Button Communication

Karen E. Mueller, DVM

Ebook: 978-1-971218-05-2

Paperback: 978-1-971218-02-1

Hardback: 978-1-971218-03-8

Disclaimer:

This book is for educational and entertainment purposes only. While every effort has been made to ensure accuracy, no warranties are expressed or implied. The author is not providing legal, financial, medical, or professional advice. External website URLs are provided for convenience; accuracy and availability are not guaranteed. The author is not responsible for losses resulting from use of the information herein.

Permissions Note:

This book references real dogs (including Bunny and Chaser) as examples of button-based communication or word learning, based on publicly available information or the author's observations. No copyrighted photographs, extended quotations, or proprietary instructional content are reproduced. Photographs of commercially available communication buttons are the author's own and are included for illustrative and educational purposes only. Each reference is brief, factual, and consistent with standard nonfiction practice.

Cover design by Wild Bloom Publishing.

First Edition 2025 · K. Mueller Publishing

Printed in the United States of America.

Dedication

For the dogs who have something to say,
and the humans who are ready to listen.

Contents

Introduction

Your dog already has a lot to say. Now it's time to help them say it clearly.

Button training isn't about teaching tricks—it's about building communication, confidence, and connection. With the guidance in these pages, you'll learn how to introduce words, avoid common mistakes, understand intentional presses, and celebrate the moments your dog surprises you with a message you never expected.

This approach is rooted in positive reinforcement—rewarding clear communication rather than correcting mistakes.

No perfection. No pressure. Just a journey you and your dog take together.

And trust me—you can do it.

*You'll also find optional bonus materials online at **KMuellerPublishing.com** to support your journey together.

Chapter 1
Rethinking Communication with Your Dog

Paddy just learning about buttons.

Years ago, I adopted a dog named Benny—a half-grown, very sick street puppy from Mexico. With time, he recovered, learned his house manners, and became an amazing family dog, but one challenge lingered: telling me when he needed to go outside. He would pace around the room, pause near the door, and occasionally whine. I tried teaching him to bark, sit by the door, or ring a bell to help give a clear signal, but he never quite caught on.

From a training perspective, it served as a reminder of the importance of clear and consistent communication. Benny was trying to express himself, but we lacked a shared language. Sound buttons could have bridged that gap beautifully, by giving him a concrete way to signal his needs and reducing both our frustration. I often think about how empowering it would have been for him to press the "outside" button instead of guessing what would make me understand him.

Benny, our extraordinary dog from Mexico.

The Button Revolution—Why Teach Your Dog to Talk?

Recently, dog button training has gone from an oddity to a global trend. Social media is overflowing with clips of dogs like Bunny communicating needs, preferences, moods, or feelings with boards of labeled buttons. These aren't mere memes; they've fostered online communities—Facebook groups, Reddit threads, and chats—all dedicated to helping owners replace the guessing game with true communication.

This movement is about more than viral videos. At its core, people yearn for clearer connections with their dogs. Button training addresses this, providing a shared system that surpasses body language or tone. Teaching your dog to press a button for "water," "play," or "cuddle" streamlines understanding and removes uncertainty. This not only simplifies daily life but also builds trust and highlights your dog's intelligence.

The benefits are far-reaching. For dogs, button use is mentally stimulating, easing boredom and anxiety—especially for those needing more engagement. A dog familiar with buttons can indicate thirst, a bathroom need, or a desire for toys without barking or pacing. For owners, it's a relief to understand requests, reduce accidents, prevent and relieve frustration, and foster more joyful moments.

Buttons create something deeper than play—they open the door to real communication. While puzzle toys offer entertainment and mental stimulation, button training builds understanding. Much like teaching words to a child, it opens a two-way channel for expressing needs and emotions. And unlike the fixed nature of puzzle toys, a soundboard can expand as your dog learns new concepts, becoming a shared, ongoing project between you. That doesn't mean you should put away the puzzle toys—they're wonderful to have as part of your dog's toybox. And when your dog is ready, add a "puzzle toy" button to their board so they can ask for playtime, too.

Practically speaking, button training can make everyday life easier. A dog in pain might press "help" or "ouch." If a stranger makes her uneasy, she could signal "stranger" or "scared." These tools allow clear communication, helping you respond accurately to your dog's needs. Over time, you may find your dog using buttons to adjust routines, request affection, or even invent creative word combinations—turning ordinary moments into genuine connection. Having your dog talk to you through buttons can feel nothing short of miraculous.

Online groups now provide spaces for advice, troubleshooting, and celebrating progress, letting owners learn from collective experience. I encourage you to draw on such resources. Whether solving a specific problem or forging a deeper bond, button training offers both structure and flexibility. With patience and curiosity, you can help your dog "speak," enriching both your lives.

Debunking the "Talking Dog" Myth—What's Real and What's Hype

The proliferation of "talking dog" videos online has sparked both awe and confusion about what dogs can do with buttons. Clips of Bunny pressing "stranger paw ouch" or appearing to ask profound questions garner millions of views, suggesting that dogs have undisclosed conversations waiting for the right technology. It's tempting to imagine any dog, with some training, could start waxing philosophical. Yet, behind these viral moments is quieter, gradual progress. Most of the time, button-trained dogs aren't making profound declarations —their "talk" is about everyday needs and routines. According to Bunny's owner, Alexis Devine, her dog's button use most often involves simple phrases like "outside," "play," and "all done."

This is consistent with research that confirms that dogs trained on soundboards do respond to words and sometimes combine buttons, and that the majority of their use is practical rather than philosophically profound.

For beginners, the first real "conversation" may be a dog pressing "water" after a walk or "outside" when needed. The beauty in these moments lies in clarity, not complexity— no guessing, no frustration—just a direct exchange. Button training offers a consistent way for your dog to communicate what matters most.

This communication isn't about grammar or complex thought, but about access, empowerment, and dependability. A "help" button allows a dog to signal discomfort or anxiety. "Cuddle" or "toy" can mean comfort, reassurance, or play. These simple exchanges hold deep meaning for both dog and owner. The focus shifts from expecting sentences to valuing every clear request, feeling, or comment.

Dispelling another myth: button training isn't just for "genius" dogs or certain breeds. Any dog—of any age, size, or ability—can learn to press buttons to express their needs.

Some owners expect instant "talking," imagining their dog will start forming sentences after a week. In reality, progress takes time, and every dog learns at their own pace. Many benefit from simple accommodations to help them succeed, such as placing buttons on a non-slip surface, adjusting the board's height, or arranging buttons to match their mobility or comfort level. (We'll cover these details later in the book.)

With patience, gentle encouragement, and your love and commitment, you can help your dog find their voice—one button at a time.

Button training isn't a miracle solution for major behavioral issues, health issues, nor a replacement for professional help for aggression. These are important issues that need to be addressed separately, and by all means, please do. Buttons are simply a practical tool for daily communication.

A good analogy is teaching sign language to toddlers. When children sign "milk" or "all done," they're requesting something they need, not reciting poetry. Your dog is doing the same—expressing their need, or telling you what they want. Some dogs may eventually string together complex thoughts, and this is largely based on the time you invest in button training and the opportunities you give them by providing buttons regularly, which will be described in detail as we go along. But the foundation always starts with basic communication — requesting what they need or want in the moment.

Regarding your training, expect some setbacks. There will be days when your dog ignores the buttons, presses randomly, or fixates on a single word. These aren't failures— they're part of learning. Having a troubleshooting mindset is key. Sometimes progress stalls until you adjust button placement, introduce different words, or wait for your dog's comfort to increase. Every mistake is a learning opportunity.

Progress isn't linear, but any press—however basic—builds connection and is an opportunity for praise.

🐾 🐾

PRE-TRAINING MINDSET CHECKLIST

Before you begin, ground yourself in realistic expectations.

☐ **Accept that progress takes time;** each dog learns at their own pace. Small, steady steps are normal for every learner.

☐ **Focus on connection, not perfection.** Your relationship matters more than flawless button presses.

☐ **Celebrate small wins** — curiosity, sniffing, or glancing all count. Early interest builds motivation and confidence.

☐ **Ditch comparisons;** your dog's journey will differ from every online video. Real life is slower, messier, and more meaningful.

☐ **Keep sessions short and positive.** End while your dog is engaged and having fun.

Remember: buttons build trust — they don't replace love, walks, or play. Approaching training with patience and perspective creates a smoother, more rewarding communication journey.

🐾 🐾

What Is AAC?

AAC—Augmentative and Alternative Communication— refers to tools that help someone express thoughts, needs, or emotions when speech isn't available. In humans, that might be a picture board, gesture system, or electronic device with recorded words or symbols. For dogs, sound buttons serve the same purpose: a consistent way to turn intention into sound.

The parallels between children using communication boards and dogs using buttons are surprisingly natural. Both rely on associative learning—linking a word, a sound, and an outcome over time. Just as a child taps a picture of a swing to say they want to play, a dog can learn that pressing "walk" makes the desired event happen. Dogs are exceptionally skilled at this type of pattern recognition, which is why they respond so well to consistent modeling and predictable outcomes.

Famous examples like Chaser—the border collie who learned the names of over a thousand objects—demonstrate that dogs can associate sounds with meaning. Ongoing studies in canine cognition continue to show how adaptable dogs are in connecting words with objects, actions, and feelings. While this doesn't mean dogs form sentences the way humans do, it confirms that intentional, meaningful communication is well within their capabilities.

AAC for dogs doesn't create poetry—it creates clarity. Just as a child pressing "book" makes their request clear, a dog pressing "walk" turns guessing into understanding. These moments build trust and reduce frustration, while giving dogs a new sense of confidence. As communication grows, behaviors like whining or pacing often decrease, giving way to calmer, more purposeful interactions. Many owners notice that button use strengthens relationships and brings more harmony to the home.

For many, the first clear button press feels like a doorway opening—the wall between species suddenly thinner.

Science can explain the process, but not the moment your dog truly connects—when a thought becomes spoken word and understanding passes between you. This quiet moment of recognition is the shared magic of AAC, whether held in a child's hand or resting beneath a dog's paw.

Chapter 2
Laying the Foundation: Before You Begin

Jimmy can hardly contain himself when it's
button training time.

Picture the look in a dog's eyes when she realizes she's finally been understood. She freezes, thinking, her gaze flicking between you and the board. Maybe it's just a hesitant paw, a soft nudge, or a breath held in concentration—but it's the first spark of connection, the moment a new kind of conversation begins.

If you doubt this will work with your dog—maybe she's older, stubborn, or not exactly a canine "Einstein"—remember that the real barrier isn't age or breed. Willingness, not pedigree or youth, is what predicts success in button training.

Breed stereotypes only add to that doubt. Many people assume certain dogs aren't suited for button training—tiny breeds for being "too yappy," or others for being "too stubborn." But everyday dogs keep proving otherwise.

My old dog, Drake, is one of them. He has arthritis and takes lots of medications and supplements. Some days he's fine; other days, every step seems to cause aches. He uses a short set of stairs to get onto the bed, but one morning, he walked to the stairs, looked up at me, then went and pressed his "help" button.

Moments like these remind us that communication isn't limited by size, age, or breed. What matters most is patience, curiosity, and trust—the foundation of every successful learner.

Every dog learns at their own speed, and progress often appears in tiny steps—sniffing or staring at a button, standing nearby, or simply watching you model the words. These moments matter; they're the quiet signs your dog is processing what comes next.

In time, even the quietest beginnings build into real communication. What feels like stillness is often your dog thinking, watching, and gathering the courage to try. Stay consistent, believe in the process, and you'll be amazed at how those early pauses transform into meaningful words.

REFLECTION SECTION: CELEBRATING MICRO-PROGRESS

After each session, jot down the faintest signs of interest. Did she glance at the button? Move closer than usual? Respond when prompted? A notebook or journal helps track moments that, over time, stack up to significant learning—even before the first successful press. The Dog Button Training Logbook: Track Your Dog's Words, Progress, and Milestones—the companion to this book—offers dedicated space for these reflections, reminders, and small achievements, because noticing progress helps keep motivation strong.

Remember, it's not a race. Button training will connect you and your dog in new ways, beyond routines or obedience cues. Focus on the connection—hoping to understand your dog better or ease daily frustrations—so you'll remain grounded as progress ebbs and flows. Celebrate every sign, no matter how small. Each press or glance is another step toward genuine conversation.

Button training is a shared journey. By setting aside doubts about age or breed and leaning into patience and consistency, you build trust, encourage learning, and discover what your dog is truly capable of.

Setting Up for Success—Choosing the Right Location

Your training environment matters almost as much as your chosen words. Like people, dogs learn best in spaces that feel secure and calm. Where you place the button board can either smooth the process or make it harder. The kitchen might seem central, but its hustle and noise can distract or overwhelm. Instead, choose a quiet spot that's close to family activity yet calm enough for focus—a living room corner often works well.

Environmental details have an outsized impact. Avoid direct sunlight; glare makes labels harder to read—mostly for the humans. Bright light and noisy electronics may discourage approach, so aim for softer light and minimal disruption. Even shifting the board a few feet away from a window or busy walkway can help your dog feel more relaxed and engaged.

Check the flooring. Slippery surfaces like hardwood can cause hesitation or slips, undermining confidence. Place a non-slip mat under the board for stability, quiet, and good footing. Rubber-backed rugs or yoga mats work well—press down yourself: if it slides, it's not secure. Sound matters too. Hard floors amplify button clicks, which can startle sensitive dogs. A rug or mat will help dampen noise and encourage exploration.

Leave enough space around the board. Your dog should be able to approach from any angle, not just straight on. This is especially important if you have multiple dogs. When the board is tucked into a corner, a dog may feel trapped, slowing progress. Give large or mobility-limited dogs extra space and raise or lower the button board placement as needed.

Ensure visual clarity. As you will learn, labels are mostly for the humans, and should be bold, high-contrast, and easy to read from a distance. Snap a quick photo of the layout—it helps everyone in the household keep track and spot misplaced buttons quickly.

ENVIRONMENTAL SETUP CHECKLIST

Creating a calm, clear space helps your dog learn with confidence.

☐ **Pick the right spot** — choose a calm area near family activity but free from clutter, glare, and noise. Choose a space where your dog can relax without constant interruptions.

☐ **Control the light** — indirect, soft light helps your dog see and focus. Avoid harsh glare or reflections that make labels difficult to read.

☐ **Control noise** — reduce background sounds and echo with rugs or mats. A quieter area helps your dog stay focused and less startled by button presses.

☐ **Check the surface** — ensure solid, non-slip footing for safe, confident button use. A stable surface prevents slipping and boosts your dog's confidence at the board.

☐ **Allow room to move** — give your dog space to approach the board comfortably from any side. Extra room helps large or mobility-limited dogs navigate more easily.

☐ **Keep labels clear** — use bold, high-contrast text. Take a quick photo so the whole family keeps the layout consistent.

A well-designed space sets your dog up for comfortable, confident learning from day one.

Visual Setup Guide

Imagine a quiet living room corner: a sturdy, non-slip mat, four evenly spaced buttons, and enough room for your dog to circle the board freely. Sunlight filters in softly, avoiding glare. A nearby chair lets you sit comfortably, while the rest of the space stays open and uncluttered. Button labels are bold and easy to read. Consider sketching a quick floor plan or snapping a photo—it's an instant reference for anyone assisting with training.

   A thoughtful setup does more than look tidy—it gives your dog comfort and confidence as she explores her new "voice." The proper layout, lighting, and surfaces can mean the difference between cautious testing and eager participation. A supportive space makes learning easier, calmer, and quicker for both of you.

Family Agreements—Getting Everyone on the Same Page for Consistent Training

When your dog learns to "talk" with buttons, she's communicating with the whole household—making consistency essential. If family members use different buttons for the same concept—such as pressing "walk" for the backyard instead of "outside," or "park" instead of "walk"— your dog will get confused. Decide together on one clear word per button, and use it consistently in both modeling and response. This shared vocabulary helps your dog form strong associations and speeds up learning.

Define clear household roles. The "training captain" leads sessions; the "button checker" ensures buttons work and stay clean; and the "progress tracker" records successes and challenges. Sharing roles prevents miscommunication and spreads the workload. If you have children, rotate duties—maybe your daughter leads training on Mondays, your partner on Wednesdays, and you on weekends—to keep everyone involved and invested.

Busy families can weave short sessions into daily routines. A family with two working parents and three kids can create a fridge chart assigning each person a "lead trainer" day to ensure everyone gets their turn. Even five-minute sessions after dinner or before school make a difference. What matters most is regularity and attention, not length. Miss a session? No worries—just pick up at the next session.

Before getting started, gather everyone and talk about your goals together. Explain why consistency matters, and invite ideas from all ages. Use simple, shared scripts such as, "We'll teach Lola the 'eat' button first, and give her a few kibbles in her bowl when she's successful at first." Write down your agreed-upon words, leadership days, and celebration ideas for milestones, then post this family plan near the button board as a cheerful reminder of your shared project.

TRAINER'S NOTE:

The "eat" and "treat" buttons are the two that get a pass from the usual "no-treating" rule of button training.

Because many dogs are highly food-motivated, these buttons can be the easiest to teach—but also the easiest to misuse. To keep things clear and consistent, drop a few kibbles or a small treat in your dog's food bowl each time "eat" or "treat" is pressed during training, rather than giving them from your hand. This reinforces the true purpose of button use for communicating—not as a cue for earning a reward.

Kids bring both excitement and challenge during button training. Competitions may arise over whose voice the dog prefers or who gets to record words. Preferably, families can make it a team adventure—switching roles and keeping learning fun. One sibling can teach "play," another "water," alternating weekly, recording voices with supervision, and tracking each first press. Kids can also try silly voices for certain words like "walkies" or "playtime" (as long as they are clearly audible) to make sessions more playful and encourage shy dogs to participate.

Naturally, families won't always stay perfectly in sync. A child might be sneaking the dog treats or prompting her outside training time, and a parent might use the wrong word or use it in the wrong context. Address inconsistencies gently, reminding everyone why they matter. If someone's interest fades—a busy older sibling, for example—invite them to help in new ways, like tracking progress or managing recordings. Flexibility keeps everyone engaged.

For recurring issues, hold brief family meetings. Review training logs, discuss what's working, and tweak strategies together. Ask: Did we use the same word? Were sessions too long? Did we reward presses right away?

Reflecting as a team strengthens your approach and ensures everyone's voice is heard.

When families coordinate cues, routines, and encouragement, dogs thrive. Button training becomes more than a task—it's a shared project that deepens bonds, builds patience, and nurtures true two-way communication.

FAMILY TEAM TRAINING CHECKLIST

Shared guidelines to help every family member support your dog's communication journey.

☐ **Agree on button words** — choose one clear word per concept; no substitutes. For example, the word for going outside to potty in the backyard is "outside," not walk, potty, or yard.

☐ **Stay consistent** — use the same word and phrasing each time when modeling or responding.

☐ **Assign family roles** — the Training Captain leads sessions, the Button Checker keeps buttons clean, and the Progress Tracker records successes and challenges.

☐ **Keep it short and regular** — even five-minute sessions help. If you miss one, simply pick up at the next session.

☐ **Involve everyone** — rotate duties so kids and adults each take turns leading, recording, or responding.

☐ **Make it fun** — switch roles, celebrate milestones, and let kids try silly voices (for certain words, as long as they're clearly audible).

☐ **Handle hiccups gently** — if someone uses the wrong word or prompts outside their training rotation, remind them kindly why consistency matters.

☐ **Reflect together** — hold quick family check-ins to review what's working and what to adjust.

Working as a coordinated team helps your dog learn faster, reduces confusion, and turns button training into a shared family victory.

Recognizing Your Dog's Unique Communication Style

Before introducing a button, take time to understand how your dog already "talks." Every dog communicates through body language, emotions, and personality. Some are expressive with tails, others with eyes or posture. Observe closely: what does your dog do to ask for food or attention? Maybe she stands by the door, circles, barks, or sits and stares. Simple notes in your logbook can help you track her language and reactions over time.

Notice vocal cues as well. Some dogs whimper for attention; others have a distinctive "play" bark that's lighter than their warning bark. You might catch sighs, grunts, or sneezes. Every sound fits a context—watch what's happening when your dog makes each noise. Do her ears perk up at certain words? Does she freeze when you reach for the leash? Keep these observations together, and you'll soon see patterns—your dog's pre-existing language.

Body language speaks volumes, too. Posture, tail set, and facial expression reveal a lot. Relaxed dogs often show relaxed jaws, soft eyes, and lips. Tense dogs show tight muscles, tense lips, and tucked tails—clear signs of stress. When your dog is relaxed and eager for something, does she shift her weight forward or glance between you and her goal? These small details matter—they reveal her intent even before she tries a button.

Think about the rhythm of your dog's day. Does she want to play after breakfast? Can you tell because she brings you a toy? If so, write it down in your log—the time, what she did, and what kind of toy. "Ball," "bone," or "rope" might be words you'll want to teach her. Does she want to nap with you before dinner? Note her mood and the time; "nap" or "cuddle" might be words you'll want to teach later. Over several days, you'll start to see reliable patterns tied to specific needs. That said, "eat" and "outside" are often the easiest to teach because dogs use them at least 2-3 times a day, every day.

Observing your dog this way is about more than gathering data; it's about understanding her perspective. You'll figure out what she enjoys and what makes her uncomfortable, allowing you to design training that stays fun and interesting.

A shared observation journal helps families coordinate their efforts. If several people care for your dog, ask each person to note what they see. A teen might notice her staring at the fridge after school, while you notice her whining at bedtime. Sharing these notes provides a fuller picture and is helpful for your initial button words.

Try keeping a daily observation log for the first week. Each day, jot down at least three signals, with their context and outcome. At the end of the week, review your notes as a family. Decide which signals repeat most often and which needs are most consistent or urgent. This process builds empathy, prepares you for training, and strengthens the bond between you and your dog.

Every dog is unique, with her own way of expressing herself. Observing, recording, and reflecting on your dog's body language is a respectful way to appreciate her individuality and communication style.

By understanding your dog's baseline "vocabulary," you create a solid foundation for button training. The patterns you record now will guide which words to teach first. With this preparation, you're ready to help your dog "speak"—and the next chapter will show how to turn today's observations into tomorrow's action. bark that's lighter than their warning bark. You might catch sighs, grunts, or sneezes. Every sound fits a context—watch what's happening when your dog makes each noise. Do her ears perk up at certain words? Does she freeze when you reach for the leash? Keep these observations together, and you'll soon see patterns—your dog's pre-existing language.

Keeping a short daily log helps you spot your dog's natural communication patterns and decide which words to teach first. Record just three or four moments a day—no need to overthink it.

TRAINING TIP: OBSERVATION LOG EXAMPLE

Sample Entries:
Time: 7:30 a.m. — Circles by door, looks at leash (right after breakfast) → Possible meaning: "Outside"
Time: 4:15 p.m. — Brings tennis ball, nudges my knee (after nap) → Possible meaning: "Play" or "Ball"
Time: 8:45 p.m. — Climbs on couch, sighs, wants in my lap

(evening routine) → Possible meaning: "Cuddle" or
"Want up"
Tip: Patterns often appear within days. Repeated cues
such as bringing a toy or circling the door, make excellent
first button words such as "ball" or "squeaky", and
"outside".

Chapter 3
Your First Buttons—A Step-by-Step Launch Plan

Paddy meets his new button for the first time.

Choosing the Perfect First Words—Needs, Wants, and Household Relevance

Imagine this: you and your dog come in from a satisfying game of fetch in the yard. You flop onto the couch while your dog pads into the kitchen for a drink. A moment later, you hear the word "water." You know the bowl was already full before you went out, so your dog isn't asking for water—she's commenting about having a drink of water! How cool is that?

Paddy and the Steak

We're a vegetarian household—have been for ages. Until recently. My husband bought meat for the first time in... well, forever. An actual steak.

I was in my office typing when Paddy trotted in, slapped the "Daddy" button, and stared at me like he had breaking news.

"Yes, Paddy—Daddy? Okay, go see Daddy!"

I called out, "Karl, call Paddy! He's asking for you!"

Karl's voice came back, strained: "I can't—I'm cooking!" (One crisis at a time.)

Paddy headed toward the kitchen with a toy in his mouth, clearly on a mission.

A few minutes later, he returned and pressed "Daddy" again, then once again left my office.

"Karl," I called, "he's talking about you—he pressed 'Daddy' again!"

Right then, Karl walked into my office—Paddy proudly

leading. Karl announced that the steak was under the broiler, the broiler was now smoking, and things had taken a dramatic turn in the kitchen.

And just as he was mid-sentence, Paddy let out a little whine and pointed his nose under my side table... where his ball was stuck.

(Thus began Crisis No. 2.)

Suddenly, everything clicked.

Yes—Paddy really had been updating me about Daddy.

And the steak.

He had thoughts. Maybe he had concerns. He was clearly reporting the situation.

But once Daddy physically arrived?

That changed the assignment entirely.

Suddenly the message became:

"Hey, Daddy... while you're here, can you get my ball?"

Because why waste a perfectly good audience with opposable thumbs?

And he did all of that with one word.

Moments like this show the power of picking the right first words. When your dog learns to express real, everyday needs, buttons become more than gadgets—they become a bridge to genuine understanding.

It helps to separate needs from wants when choosing first words. Needs include basics like "outside," "water," or "eat"—essentials for comfort and safety. These requests are consistent, urgent, and provide reliable teaching moments. Wants, like "ball" or "bone," are fun but less essential.

Starting with needs tends to yield quicker, more reliable results. Because they occur frequently throughout the day, they offer more natural teaching opportunities—and they're not optional. Prioritizing needs also builds trust: your dog learns that you consistently meet those basic requests, while wants may come and go from day to day.

Consider what truly excites your dog, and take the time to observe her daily life. What is she trying to tell you? Those natural signals are your best clues. If "walk" makes her dance with excitement, or she bolts to the door when you say "outside," those are ideal starter words.

They're familiar and easy to practice several times a day. Frequent repetition—paired with plenty of modeling (we'll talk about that soon)—speeds learning and keeps both of you engaged.

If you're unsure where to begin, try a quick household audit. Spend a day or two simply watching your dog's patterns. Note routines she repeats—waiting at the door, sitting by the bowl, bringing toys to you. Ask family members what they've noticed, too; everyone sees different details. Comparing notes helps reveal the most meaningful and useful first words, as well as words for later on.

Although it might seem easier to start with a single word, dogs actually learn faster when you introduce a small set. They understand language through comparison and context. Begin with four to six practical words—such as "outside," "water," "eat," and "play"—that fit naturally into daily routines and allow frequent practice. With only one or two words, there's less context to learn from, and progress tends to move more slowly.

As your dog starts to understand and respond to those first buttons, you can gradually expand to "want" words like "ball" or "bone." Just remember: clear, consistent results keep learning strong.

Avoid abstract or emotional phrases early on. Sweet words like "I love you" or "friend" don't produce clear, concrete outcomes. Without a visible result, your dog can lose interest or become confused. Start with words that lead to action—opening a door, giving water, offering food, or starting a game—and build from there. Tangible success is what keeps communication exciting and rewarding for both of you.

Next, narrow your shortlist by considering your dog's strongest motivations. Ball-obsessed dogs may thrive with "play" or "ball," while food-motivated dogs might start best with "eat" or "treat." Choose words that reflect your dog's real priorities—not what's popular online.

Every home is different. A quiet household with a rescue dog will have other priorities than a bustling family with two energetic retrievers. Tailor your button choices to your dog's actual life and environment.

Most importantly, stay observant and willing to adapt. The best first words are the ones that truly matter to your dog and fit naturally into your daily routines. This thoughtful, customized start lays the groundwork for communication that's not only successful but also meaningful as your dog's vocabulary grows.

CHECKLIST: CHOOSING YOUR FIRST WORDS

Run through this checklist before picking your starter buttons.

☐ **Clear Reaction:** Does the word already elicit a clear reaction from my dog?

☐ **Daily Practice:** Can I practice this word several times daily?

☐ **Actionable Meaning:** When my dog uses this button, do I know what action to take?

☐ **Recognizable Behaviors:** Does my dog have specific behaviors tied to this word? (For example: brings the leash for "walk," goes to the door for "outside," sits by the bowl for "water.")

☐ **Household Friendly:** Is this word easy and relevant for the whole household to reinforce?

If you answered yes to most of these, you've found a strong candidate for your first set of buttons.

Button Selection Demystified—Comparing Features of Talking Buttons

Choosing talking buttons can feel overwhelming at first, but this guide should help. If possible, start by checking your local pet stores; then, look online as well. You might find the ideal buttons or boards online, but your neighborhood pet store is still a great place to pick up toys, poop bags, batteries, and other supplies. Supporting local shops provides jobs, keeps your dollars in the community, and helps ensure those stores are still there when you need them.

When shopping for buttons, focus on your dog's

abilities and comfort. Larger buttons often work well for big dogs who press with enthusiasm. In comparison, smaller buttons are suitable for petite breeds, lighter paws, or tighter spaces. Ultimately, the best choice is whatever lets your dog press confidently and consistently. The goal is to select buttons that make pressing them easy and natural, without requiring extra effort.

Avoid the cheapest option available. Most buttons on the market are simple tools, but consistency and clarity still matter. Prioritize buttons with crisp, distinct sounds; fuzzy or tinny recordings can make learning more difficult. Durability matters too—buttons that jam or break quickly lead to frustration for both trainer and dog. Keep in mind, these buttons are simple tools, not high-end electronics.

Starter packs, often with four to six buttons, are ideal for beginners. They usually come with setup guides, making them practical when you're just starting. When ready for more words, brands offering small packs of buttons make expansion easier. Choose brands that are compatible with modular mats, if possible, for neat and organized growth. (For a deeper dive into popular button types and their advantages, see Chapter 11.)

Labeling is another important feature. Some brands offer stickers, while others require a DIY approach, such as using tape. Well-labeled buttons help you and your dog identify each word, streamlining the learning process.

Consider the power source as well. Most buttons use replaceable batteries for quick swaps, while USB-rechargeable models eliminate the need for batteries but require regular charging, which can be challenging once your setup grows. For busy households or those that travel frequently, choose the option that best fits your lifestyle.*

Noise level is another factor to consider. Some buttons are surprisingly loud and can startle sensitive dogs. Seek quieter models if your dog is easily spooked. Reading reviews or checking online communities can offer helpful, real-world feedback—especially if your dog has special needs or sensitivities.

Above all, favor accessibility over fancy features. Your dog should be able to use her buttons independently. Always consider her size, mobility, and strength before setting up. The best button is the one your dog can use easily and confidently—day after day.

*A Word About Battery Recycling

Batteries are some of the worst things to end up in a landfill—and some of the easiest to recycle once you know where to take them. They can leak acid and heavy metals, which are toxic to soil, water, and wildlife. In the Pacific Northwest, Ridwell is one organization that accepts batteries, along with other hard-to-recycle items such as light bulbs and plastics. You can learn more about their great program at www.ridwell.com. If your local recycling program doesn't take batteries, check for nearby drop-off locations or small battery shops that do. Keeping batteries out of the trash protects pets, wildlife, and our environment.

Button Accessibility — Final Checklist

Use this quick self-assessment to confirm your dog's button setup is comfortable and accessible.

☐ **Reachability:** My dog can reach each button from all directions without stretching or needing assistance.

☐ **Mobility-Friendly Setup:** For dogs with arthritis, joint stiffness, or limited movement, buttons are reachable without strain.

☐ **Noise Sensitivity:** The sound level suits my dog—loud enough for me to hear, but not startling for her.

☐ **Secure Flooring:** The flooring around the buttons is either not slippery, or I have placed non-slip material to prevent slipping.

☐ **Stable Buttons:** Buttons stay firmly in place and don't slide or tip when pressed.

With an accessible setup in place, your dog can use her buttons independently and reliably as her vocabulary grows.

Set Up and Recording Your Buttons

This is the exciting part—you've got your first four to six buttons, and you're ready to record them. No worries—you've got this! Grab your batteries or charging cord and dive in. Most buttons use two AAA batteries and a small screwdriver for installation. The record button is usually located on the side; press and hold it, say your word clearly, then release. That's it! Now press the button, just as your dog would, to double-check the sound.

Your voice is everything to your dog—and tone really counts. The energy and emotion you record is what your dog will hear and respond to. Even if you're naturally soft-spoken, this is the time to use your "happy voice." Say each word the way you'll actually use it with your dog, and practice a few times before recording. Try to keep your volume consistent from one button to the next. Some buttons may play back slightly louder or softer than others, so adjust your voice as needed to keep them sounding even and inviting.

Dogs naturally respond to energy and emotion. An enthusiastic "Outside!" will grab your dog's attention far more than a flat or hesitant tone. Let your voice reflect your dog's excitement—if she loves "walk" or "play," let that joy shine through naturally. You don't need to shout; a warm, upbeat tone builds connection, curiosity, and motivation.

Mistakes happen while recording—so don't stress. A lawnmower might start mid-recording, a truck might drive by, or you might cough. Most buttons can be re-recorded easily. Sometimes a word doesn't sound as clear as you'd like, so take a moment to listen and try again. You want the word to sound the way you actually say it to your dog—bright, natural, and easy to recognize. Even high-quality buttons can sound a little fuzzy or distorted, so take your time, speak slowly and clearly, and keep that happy tone your dog already loves.

Consistency builds learning. Try to use the same person's voice for each word, especially for key buttons like "outside" and "food." If several people want to help, and you're using multiple buttons for the same word, assign specific words to each person. Dogs notice vocal patterns, and sudden changes in voice can create hesitation or confusion.

If you ever struggle to get a clear recording—or if you simply want perfectly crisp, consistent audio every time—an AI voice can help. It removes background noise, evens out volume, and gives you smooth pronunciation without the pressure of getting your own voice "just right." Many handlers find that a steady, uniform voice helps their dog distinguish words more easily.

Using CapCut to Record Button Audio (Easy Play-By-Play)
- Download and open the CapCut app. It's free in the App Store or Google Play.
- Start a new project (or use any blank project).
- Type in the word or phrase you want your button to say (e.g., play, all done, dental chew).
- Choose an AI voice you like and preview your options.
- Adjust the speed or tone if needed—steady, clear audio works best.
- Play the audio from your phone. You don't have to export anything unless you want to.
- Hold your phone near the button's microphone.
- Press and hold the record button on your talking button while the AI voice plays the word.
- Release the record button when the audio finishes.
- Test your button and re-record if the sound is muffled or clipped.

RECORDING REVIEW: QUICK CHECKLIST

Before moving on, make sure recordings sound clear, natural, and consistent.
☐ **Quiet Environment:** Background sounds (like TVs, phones, and music) are off.

☐ **Clean Edges:** Brief pauses before and after the word prevent the beginning or end from getting cut off.

☐ **Balanced Volume:** Sound is loud enough to hear easily, gentle enough not to startle.

☐ **Quality Check:** Play back, and re-record if needed. A clear, upbeat recording helps your dog recognize your voice and stay engaged in learning.

With clear recordings in place, your dog can start learning confidently from the very first press.

First Button Placement—Solutions for Any Home Layout

Button placement shapes your dog's learning speed and confidence. Accessibility and relevance are key. Place the button beside the outcome it triggers—for "outside," set it by the main door your dog uses for walks, linking location to action for easy understanding. For a "toy" button, move toys or the toy box nearby so pressing is immediately rewarded with play.

Reduce distractions by avoiding crowded, noisy, or cluttered spots. Don't place buttons in hallways or by TVs where they might be trampled or ignored. Find a quiet, central area—close to where your dog relaxes and spends time, but free of obstacles.

There are two main approaches to button placement, and the first is to position a few buttons near important areas used several times daily, such as the door, food dish, water bowl, or toy box. This setup is especially helpful for puppies who need to go outside quickly or for dogs still learning their first words. It provides frequent, natural training opportunities and makes learning easier in specific home layouts.

The second approach is to group buttons on a single board in a central area of the home—often the living room, a large entryway, an open kitchen, or a den. This allows your dog to access her "vocabulary" in one place and encourages communication during daily family routines.

Whenever possible, ensure the board can be reached from all directions so your dog can access her buttons comfortably, regardless of her direction of approach.

Using boards keeps buttons organized in a consistent location, and makes them easy to move. As your dog's vocabulary grows, try to keep her most important words together on one or two boards that you can move around the house or take on trips. This helps maintain consistency and provides your dog with a reliable way to communicate with you, wherever you go.

Layout considerations apply to every home. In houses with open plans, place the board in the central living area or wherever family activity takes place. In multi-exit homes, put the "outside" button by the door your dog uses the most. For homes with multiple floors, place the main buttons on the level with the most daily routines. Sketches or diagrams can help you visualize placement.

Consistency in placement is essential. Dogs associate meaning with a button's location even more than with its appearance, so moving buttons can lead to confusion or setback. Label each button's spot with stickers or tape so it's easy to return them to their original position after cleaning or rearranging. Always keep the board in the same orientation. A stable layout helps your dog learn faster and builds confidence in using their words.

Safety should never be overlooked. Ensure the board and surrounding area are slip-resistant so neither the board nor your dog slips during use. A non-skid rug or mat under the board works well on smooth floors. If buttons come loose, secure them with Velcro to keep them in place and avoid frustration. Keep the board and its surrounding area clean, dry, and clutter-free. Tidy any cords or cables, and replace batteries as needed. Be sure spent batteries are safely stored until they are recycled or disposed of.

Before settling on a location, perform an Accessibility Test. Watch your dog approach the board: can she reach it easily and from more than one direction? If she hesitates, adjust height or angle. Smaller or older dogs may require a tilted or wall-mounted setup, while taller dogs may benefit from a low platform. Make minor tweaks until your dog uses the board comfortably. An accessible, inviting setup encourages curiosity and use. Over time, your dog will integrate button use into her daily routine—returning again and again, each press strengthening trust and skill.

Above all, placement isn't just about convenience. It's about creating a welcoming space where your dog feels invited to communicate. The correct location turns buttons into natural tools for everyday conversation.

Button Placement Checklist

Before you begin modeling or recording, use this checklist to make sure your dog's buttons are placed where she can succeed—easy to reach, safe, and inviting to use.

☐ **Place buttons where they make sense.** For example, "outside" near the main door your dog uses most, or "eat" near the food bowl.

☐ **Choose calm locations.** Avoid hallways, cluttered rooms, and noisy areas like TVs or speakers.

☐ **If possible, make the board reachable** from all directions. Your dog should be able to approach the board from several directions.

☐ **Adjust for size and mobility.** Small or older dogs may need a tilted or wall-mounted board; tall dogs, a low platform.

☐ **Be consistent.** Label each button's spot and always return the board to the same orientation.

☐ **Prevent slipping on smooth floors.** Use a non-skid rug for both your dog and the button board to prevent slipping.

☐ **Keep it clean and safe.** Keep buttons indoors, clean, and dry. Tidy cords and cables, and change batteries as needed.

☐ **Stay flexible.** Portable boards let you move key words around the house—or take them when you travel.

Setting your dog up with safe, sensible button placement ensures early success and builds confident communication from the very start.

Chapter 4
The First Press: Jumpstarting Communication

Jimmy enthusiastically hits a different button.

This is where everything starts to come together. Your modeling, patience, and consistency begin to take shape in small but exciting ways. Every glance toward the board, every pause beside a button, is progress toward real communication.

Whether your dog is cautious or bold, progress starts quietly. You might notice her staring at a button, sniffing it, or even stepping on it by accident. These early moments matter. They're the bridge between observation and communication—the small, unremarkable beginnings that lead to that unforgettable first press.

Training Tip:

If you don't already have the *Dog Button Training Logbook—a companion journal to Button Training for Dogs* by the same author—consider getting it now as you begin introducing buttons. It's the perfect place to start recording your early sessions. Note which words you've introduced, how often you model them, and how your dog responds. Over time, these notes reveal patterns you might otherwise miss: growing curiosity, increased confidence, and the first signs of independent presses.

Modeling Words for Your Dog—Learning by Imitating

Picture yourself getting your dog's meal ready while she watches intently, tail wagging in anticipation. Dogs learn best by observing and mirroring daily life—not just through direct teaching. Modeling means saying a word and showing its meaning so your dog begins to link sounds with actions. In this case, you might be talking to your dog about her breakfast and emphasizing the word *eat*. Then, when you introduce buttons, the first word you might choose is *eat*. For button training, modeling means pressing a button and saying the chosen word or phrase just before or after the press to reinforce its meaning.

A helpful guideline is to model a word three times in one round of modeling—say the word, press the button, and link it to the action three separate times. These quick, repeated pairings give your dog a strong, unmistakable association. Research in both animal learning and early language development shows that learners form stronger connections when they hear or see a new word several times in the same window of time. Repeating the word and its button three times gives your dog clear links between sound, action, and meaning—and that repetition helps the word sink in.

A higher-pitched, melodic tone—often called 'parentese'—naturally captures your dog's attention. Speak slowly, raise your pitch slightly, and exaggerate your tone. Instead of a flat "water," try a cheerful "waa-ter! Want "water"?" Dogs respond more readily to warmth and enthusiasm, making learning feel fun and rewarding for both of you.

Modeling gives your dog consistent word-button

connections, much like how parents teach toddlers new words. Progress takes time; most dogs need weeks or even months before using buttons consistently. Keep sessions short and natural—just a few minutes woven into daily life. These small, frequent moments build strong associations without overwhelming either of you.

Start with your four to six previously chosen, important words and weave them into everyday routines. Your dog learns from you repeating the word before, during, and after each action—just as babies learn through repeated exposure to words in context. At breakfast, talk about and press eat as you serve food, and talk about and press "water" before you refill the bowl, while you're refilling it, and right after you finish. Over time, your dog will connect each button to the words that matter most to them.

Model each word several times a day for two to three weeks before expecting your dog to press independently. Watch for natural prompts—your dog waiting by the door, standing at her bowl, or eyeing her toy—and use those moments for modeling. After pressing the button and saying the word, pause for up to thirty seconds—or even sixty, if she needs it. That quiet moment gives her time to think, make sense of what she saw, and even try pressing on her own.

EXAMPLE: MODELING "WATER" THROUGHOUT THE DAY

Your modeling of the word "water" might look something like this in an everyday routine. In the morning, you might say, "Riley, want some "water"?" and press the "water" button once. As you walk to the sink, press the "water" button again and say, "I'm getting your "water" now." When you pour it into his dish, press the "water" button a third time and say, "Here is your "water"!"

Using the word—and the button—three times in a single round of modeling gives your dog a clear, memorable link between sound and action.

You'll repeat this same pattern throughout the day. At lunch you might ask, "Do you want "water," Riley?" and press the button as you fill the bowl. At dinner you can say, "I'm putting "water" in your food—it makes great gravy. Want "water" to drink?" and model the button at each step of the routine.

Opportunities to model "water" appear all day long. Talk about "water" when you water your plants, wash your hands, take a shower, or refill your own glass. The more consistently your dog hears the word paired with real actions —and sees the button pressed several times—the faster the meaning takes hold. Soon, Riley will notice how often the word appears around the house and build a solid understanding of what "water" means.

Motivating Reserved Learners—Gentle Techniques for Shy Dogs

Some dogs are naturally hesitant. If your dog hangs back from the buttons or seems uninterested, don't push. Instead, make the button area inviting—sit nearby, offer gentle pats, toss toys close to the board, or simply share quiet time together. These positive moments gradually draw your dog in. When she sniffs or glances toward the buttons, praise instantly. This process, called shaping, rewards small steps forward; steps that ultimately will lead to a full press.

Sound-sensitive dogs need extra reassurance. Place the button in a quiet, cozy spot. Lower the playback volume or cushion the sound by adding felt or fabric under the button. Even covering the speaker lightly with tape or cloth can help reduce the tone's startling effect. Minor adjustments like these help timid dogs feel more secure when approaching the buttons.

Drake, a shy, observant senior learner, sniffs the buttons.

Avoid common traps—over-prompting, showing frustration, or pushing too hard. If you catch yourself repeating cues, pause, step back, and let your dog set the pace. Frustration blocks learning, especially for sensitive or independent dogs. Gentle patience and calm repetition build confidence far more effectively than pressure ever will.

Training Techniques to Avoid—Starting Right

In your eagerness to teach your dog to "talk," it's natural to want to speed things up—perhaps by coaxing her with treats or luring her with her favorite toy. Many owners try these shortcuts, hoping for that first exciting press. However, treating with food or using toys as lures teaches your dog to expect rewards for actions rather than for actual communication. Instead of linking the button with "outside" or "water," she learns to press for a reward, missing the real purpose. This often leads to frustration—she may stop pressing if the treat isn't offered or press only when she wants a reward. Dogs are smart and repeat what's reinforced. If pressing brings treats, they'll press for treats, not to communicate.

Forcing your dog's paw onto a button—even gently—creates a different problem. Imagine someone pushing your hand onto an unfamiliar device: at best, you'd be puzzled; at worst, uneasy or scared. Dogs quickly form negative associations. When pushed, they may view the buttons as stressful instead of fun. Trust is delicate—once lost, it takes time to rebuild.

Instructing your dog to "touch" or "press" the button may seem harmless, especially if she already knows those cues. But it limits her understanding—she'll interact only when prompted, missing the goal of pressing to express a want or need. Later, when you hope for independent use, you may find her waiting for direction. This habit is tough to undo and can turn buttons into props for tricks rather than tools for conversation.

Real communication is rooted in respecting your dog's natural curiosity and independence. Let her interact with the

44

buttons voluntarily, praising her for interest—not compliance. This allows for more authentic learning and discovery for both of you.

Practice for Busy Lives—3-6 Minute Session Templates

Even busy days can include productive button practice through short sessions. No big time blocks required—set aside three to six minutes, two to three times a day. Integrate these sessions before breakfast, after a walk, or during quiet evenings. Keep them light and upbeat. When your dog shows curiosity, respond with genuine joy—"good girl!" or "good boy!"—so the buttons always carry positive associations.

When your dog signals a need, use that moment to model the relevant button. Press "outside" or "water" before meeting the need to strengthen the word–action link. Repeat this throughout the day at meals, bathroom breaks, walks, or play. These consistent, meaningful moments show your dog that words hold real meaning.

Watch for small changes—these subtleties matter. Maybe she lingers by the board or glances at you after a session. After modeling a word, pause for about thirty seconds to give her time to process or try pressing on her own. That moment of patience is crucial. If she presses, celebrate—even accidental attempts count. If not, move on without stress.

Set reasonable goals and track your sessions in your button-training logbook or preferred app. Note practiced words, frequency, and your dog's reactions. Logging builds motivation and helps you spot progress. Encourage everyone in the household to participate so cues stay consistent. Celebrate every achievement—the first press deserves a photo, a mini-party, or at least a proud text to friends. Recognition keeps the energy high for learning.

Different Dogs Learn Differently

Every dog brings unique instincts and learning patterns. Your dog's response to the soundboard may not mirror a neighbor's—or a viral internet dog's—and that's completely fine. Some dogs quietly observe, taking in your routines and actions. They may seem uninterested at first, hanging back as you model button words, but they're processing. Their learning style is patient and subtle. Once they start pressing, their interactions tend to be thoughtful and deliberate.

For these observers, allow extra time after modeling. Pause, gesture encouragement, and speak softly ("It's OK, you can do it") while giving her a moment to think. That small, patient pause is powerful—it helps her process and build confidence. If nothing happens, simply carry on. Being near the board or sharing calm moments nearby helps normalize the buttons and increases the accidental presses that can be rewarded.

By contrast, exploratory learners are bold and curious from the start. They investigate, paw, or even nibble at the buttons—sometimes chaotically. This early "babbling" phase, marked by random presses or multiple hits, may look messy but is actually valuable practice. Praise it. Model the word that matches the pressed button and encourage their enthusiasm. If your dog presses indiscriminately, focus on reinforcing one word at a time. Over time, the randomness fades and purposeful presses emerge. Exploratory types thrive on feedback, so respond positively and immediately.

Button training works for all types. Observers may take

longer but often become precise, thoughtful communicators. Explorers might be messier at first, but they quickly begin to recognize patterns and meaning through repetition and feedback. Adjust your support accordingly: give space to the cautious, channel energy for the bold, and celebrate every small success.

Chapter 5
Understanding Setbacks — Moving Forward Again

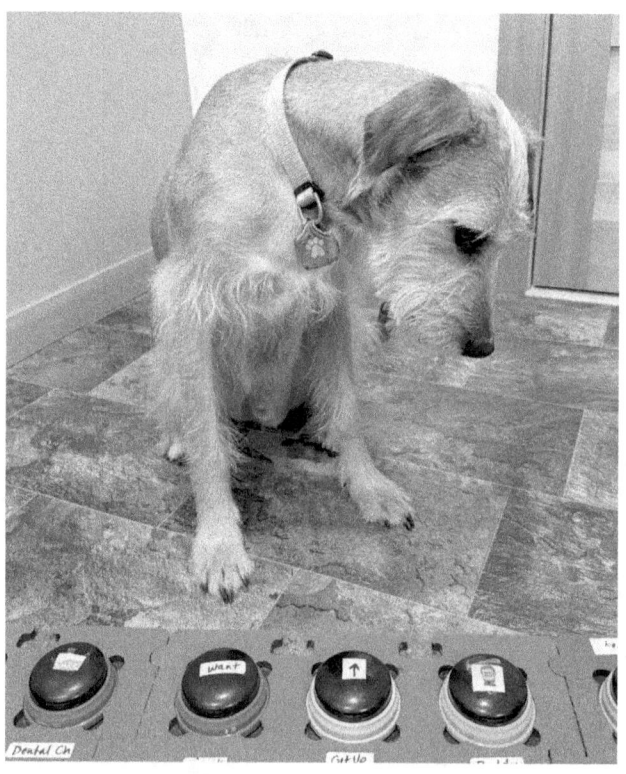

Paddy showing disinterest in the buttons.

My Dog Ignores the Button

The first weeks of button training can feel like waiting for a show that never starts. Many families eagerly set out the button board, hoping their dog will investigate, only to watch as the dog ignores it. If this sounds familiar, don't worry—you're not alone. This isn't stubbornness or a lack of intelligence; it's just a communication gap. Let's explore why it happens and how to spark your dog's interest.

Location matters. If the button is hidden behind furniture or tucked in a cramped corner, your dog might skip it or avoid the spot if it feels unwelcoming. The button should be in a place that is easy and comfortable for your dog to access from multiple angles. Try seeing the world from your dog's height; check for clear sight-lines, accessible space, and ease of movement. Make sure both you and your dog, especially if one has mobility concerns, can reach the button effortlessly. (If you're not sure, review the Button Placement Checklist at the end of Chapter 3, for detailed placement guidelines.)

Timing is another key factor. Training when your dog is tired, full, or distracted usually leads to disinterest. Find moments when your dog is awake yet calm—mid-morning or just after light play often works well. Keep training sessions short (about three to six minutes) and end them on a positive note. Consistent timing helps your dog anticipate training and stay engaged.

Inconsistent family modeling also creates hurdles. If each person uses different words or tones or presses the button at random, it confuses your dog. In the early stages, your dog is easily overwhelmed by mixed signals, so clear, consistent input matters most. Appoint one "button captain" to lead all training during the first week. This person should handle every press and prompt to keep the pattern predictable. If you have very eager family members, let the captain assign each person one word in the second week— just one—to keep things structured and easy to follow. Once your dog makes their first press, you can gradually relax the rules and allow others in more freely, since your dog will start to understand the concept of button communication.

If the button doesn't capture your dog's interest or the first words aren't meaningful, your dog may ignore them. Early success depends on motivation. Choose words that connect to something your dog already loves—like "treat," "walk," or "play." These carry emotional weight and natural curiosity. When the first word sparks excitement, your dog learns that pressing the button makes good things happen. That clear cause-and-effect is the foundation of button communication. (See the checklist in Chapter 3, Choosing Your First Words, for guidance on selecting effective starter words.)

If your dog still isn't showing interest after trying those starter words, shift your focus from needs to wants. Typically, we start with words that meet your dog's basic **needs**—things like "outside," "walk," and "eat." But if your dog isn't engaging with those, try a few that reflect what your dog **wants,** such as "toy," "treat," or "park." These words often spark stronger curiosity and motivation. Remember to praise any attempt toward a press with genuine enthusiasm, and always follow through immediately with the promised action. Repeat if possible; repetition builds understanding. (Don't offer the button unless you're ready and able to respond right away—for example, don't offer the button for "park" unless you're prepared to go to the park.)

Anxiety can also cause disinterest. Some dogs are cautious around unfamiliar objects or new sounds. If your dog seems uneasy, check the environment first. Avoid placing the button near loud appliances, high-traffic areas, or echoing corners. If the button's sound is sharp or startles your dog, try muffling it slightly with fabric or, if possible, adjust the volume. Move the button to a comfortable, familiar spot, and pair its presence with calm praise or gentle play. As your dog relaxes, curiosity will naturally follow.

When addressing avoidance, make one change at a time. When trying to figure out what's causing anxiety or avoidance, focus on one variable—such as the button's location, surface, or sound. Change only one thing at a time, then give your dog a few days to adjust before trying something else. This careful, step-by-step approach helps you pinpoint what's triggering discomfort and prevents overwhelming your dog. Over time, you'll start to see which conditions make your dog feel most relaxed and willing to engage.

Celebrate every tiny sign of interest. A glance, a sniff, or a brief pause near the button is progress. Offer gentle praise or affection to reinforce curiosity. In button training, avoid using treats—this stage is about communication, not reward expectation. Each positive experience builds your dog's comfort and confidence. Over time, curiosity becomes exploration, and exploration becomes engagement. Keep sessions brief, positive, and focused on your dog's enjoyment. Communication grows through small, steady steps, and patience always pays off.

Keep sessions brief, positive, and focused on your dog's enjoyment. Communication grows through small, steady steps—sometimes a simple change, like moving the button or adding a favorite word, turns disinterest into engagement.

Celebrate each success, no matter how small, and be patient; your dog's curiosity and confidence will continue to grow.

INTERACTIVE CHECKLIST: DIAGNOSING BUTTON AVOIDANCE

Use this quick troubleshooting list to identify why your dog might be hesitant to approach or press her buttons.

☐ **Is the button accessible** from your dog's favorite spot?
☐ **Can your dog approach** from multiple directions?
☐ **Is the area well-lit** and roomy?
☐ **Are you training** when your dog is alert and calm?
☐ **Is the same person** leading and using consistent cues?
☐ **Have you included** engaging, meaningful words and activities?
☐ **Is the environment quiet** and comfortable, with minimal distractions?
☐ **Are you changing only one thing** at a time to monitor progress?

Each day, use this list to note what you adjust. Over time, patterns will emerge—certain times, locations, or activities that boost interest. This simple log helps you fine-tune how you train, be consistent, and make training more engaging.

False Positives and Accidental Presses—What They Mean and How to Respond

Every dog learning buttons will sometimes press them unintentionally. A dog may step on "outside" while stretching or nudge "treat" out of curiosity. These false positives aren't true communication; they're just moving around in a confined space or normal exploring. Your response shapes learning.

Distinguish between planned and accidental presses. Honest communication fits the moment: your dog stands at the door, looks at you, and presses "outside." Accidental presses lack context—a stray paw during play or a wandering nose across the board. Noticing the difference prevents confusion and keeps random presses from being reinforced.

Handle accidental presses calmly. Unless your dog is nervous and needs gentle encouragement, stay neutral—don't respond or draw attention. Ignoring accidental presses teaches that button-mashing doesn't work. Avoid scolding or moving your dog away; simply let it pass. Anxious dogs may benefit from soft praise for approaching the board, but reinforcing random presses slows progress for most dogs.

Save reinforcement for deliberate, context-driven presses. When your dog presses "outside" by the door, respond immediately—open the door, praise her, and make the connection clear. Quick, consistent reactions help your dog link each word to a predictable outcome. When she taps "water" near her bowl or "play" before a game, respond with enthusiasm and note it. These meaningful moments build understanding.

Patience and repetition are essential. Dogs need many exposures before pressing with intent becomes routine. Follow the same rule each time: meaningful presses get an immediate response; random ones get ignored. This shaping —reinforcing only targeted actions—helps communication emerge. Keep modeling by pressing the matching button before each event. Consistent patterns build comprehension.

Track all presses—accidental or deliberate—to monitor progress. Use a simple log to note what was pressed, when, and in what context. For example: "Pressed 'outside' at 10 a.m. by the door," or, "Pressed 'treat' during play; ignored." Over time, patterns appear—certain words become reliable, and intentional communication becomes easier to spot.

Expect ups and downs. Some days bring random presses; other days, clear communication. Dogs may even regress briefly, tapping buttons for the fun of the sound, then return to excellent timing on "outside" or "water." These fluctuations are normal. Stay steady—reward purposeful presses and stay calm through the noise.

When you're unsure whether a press is intentional, look for clues. Eye contact, standing in a known request spot, or other anticipatory behaviors help you interpret meaning. With practice, reading your dog's signals becomes instinctive, allowing you to reinforce real communication.

Consistency is crucial. Dogs learn best when expectations remain steady. Only reward presses that match the context—otherwise, your dog may try all the buttons hoping for a prize. Logging keeps everyone on the same page about what seems intentional. With time, clear feedback and consistent rules help button presses evolve into actual conversations.

Overcoming Button Shyness—Desensitization for Nervous or Senior Dogs

Some dogs shy away, freeze, or leave the room at the slightest sound of a button. Seniors, anxious dogs, and rescues may find the button more intimidating than interesting. Flinching, tail tucks, or wide, nervous eyes are clear indicators. Sometimes just placing the button down causes hesitation, or a rescue dog might cower at hearing the recorded voice. Button shyness isn't always obvious—watch for subtle shifts: a normally confident dog avoiding the area, circling the button, or pausing before crossing the room. Even brief glances or long hesitations signal discomfort. Read these cues as sensitively as you would with a human friend— go gently, don't rush, and avoid pressure.

Start by separating the button from its sound. Place the button near your dog's favorite spot—her bed, a sunny rug, or a cozy corner. Don't ask her to press it or expect any interaction; just let the button exist near her space. For several days, relax nearby and let your dog sniff, look at, or ignore it—any neutral or positive interaction counts as progress.

When she's comfortable around the silent button, muffle the sound and press it with your hand from a distance so she can gradually get used to it. If the sound is too loud, muffling it with tape or felt can help. For very anxious dogs, this is one situation where intermittent treats can help. Press the muffled button from across the room, then walk to her to offer gentle reassurance. Move away again, press the button, then return to her calmly. This slow back-and-forth rhythm helps her pair the sound with safety and support. If she startles or leaves, stay relaxed and avoid direct eye contact—

she's learning that the sounds on the button are not threatening. As she remains calm, gradually decrease the distance over several days. With time, the button's sound becomes familiar rather than startling.

Dogs with physical or sensory limitations may need accommodations to help them succeed. If pressing is difficult due to arthritis or limited mobility, elevate or stabilize the buttons so she doesn't need to bend or strain to press them.

For dogs with impaired sight or hearing, keep button placement consistent and offer simple tactile cues. Adjust the setup to match your dog's abilities; the goal is to make the button easy and comfortable to use.

For dogs more confident with their nose than their paws, it may be helpful to first clicker-train them to touch a target stick with their nose before asking them to touch a button with it. Most dogs learn this readily. That said, button training is not clicker training, and this is the only time targeting is used. For a solid reference on target training—and a reliable target stick to practice with—see *The Dog Tricks and Training Workbook, Revised and Expanded* (March 18, 2025) by Kyra Sundance, and the Terry Ryan Click Stick by Karen Pryor. Both are widely available online if not at local stores.

Help your dog form positive associations by placing the button near familiar, comfortable areas—such as her bed, a blanket, or a favorite toy. Sit nearby as she settles, and keep the button within view. Offer gentle encouragement and praise when she looks at the button or shows interest in it. Any attention or movement toward the button is a step in the right direction. With your steady enthusiasm and consistency, you're shaping her behavior toward pressing the buttons.

Your environment plays a role as well. Avoid sudden

movements or loud noises during practice. Keep things low-key—quiet background sound, softer lighting, and unhurried movements. Many dogs are more likely to explore the button during quiet times of the day. You can also experiment with locations: some dogs do better in smaller, cozier spaces, while others prefer more room. Choose the setup that helps your dog stay relaxed.

Patience makes a difference. For nervous or senior dogs, comfort builds gradually. Look for practical signs of progress—a brief pause near the button, a sniff, or choosing to stay nearby. Avoid comparing your dog with friends' dogs or those you see in online groups. Every dog moves at a different pace. With consistent support, most dogs become more comfortable and more willing to interact. Each small step forward lays the foundation for calmer, more trusting communication between you and your dog.

Handling Frustration—Mindset Shifts for Slow Progress and Plateaus

If you feel like progress has stalled, you're not alone. Even dedicated trainers hit occasional walls. The early excitement fades, and suddenly days—or even weeks—go by with little visible progress. It's easy to wonder, "What am I doing wrong?" But plateaus aren't failures; they're a normal part of the process for both you and your dog. Looking back, even those "quiet" weeks—when your journal notes say only, "Looked at button; walked away"—are laying foundations beneath the surface.

It helps to redefine what success really looks like. Button training isn't about checking off milestones quickly or impressing anyone online. Real progress happens in micro-moments: a glance at the button, a sniff, a paw lifting, or simply waiting near the board. Sometimes your dog looks at you and the button in the same moment—that's a win. Track these "mini-wins" with a simple chart. Note things like "looked," "sniffed," "pawed at," or "waited nearby." These behaviors are forward motion. Celebrate them—say "good job" or offer a gentle scratch. Recognizing these steps helps keep motivation alive for both of you.

Comparison steals joy—focus on your own pace instead. Online, it can seem like everyone else's dog is "talking" overnight—stringing words together with magical ease. But those are highlight reels, not the whole story. You don't see their slow days, missed presses, or long pauses. Your dog has their own pace, your home has its own rhythm, and your journey isn't supposed to look like anyone else's. If you start feeling discouraged, reach out to the community for perspective—but keep your focus on your own path. When frustration spikes, write down three signs of engagement, even tiny ones like sitting near the board. Tell yourself, "We progress at our pace, and every step counts." This mindset keeps you grounded and patient.

Sometimes you both need a reset. When you're stuck, break the pattern. Have a "fun only" day with your dog's favorite activities and forget the buttons completely. Shifting the mood often reignites curiosity. Try training at a different time of day or in a new spot. And don't be afraid to take a week off—rest can spark renewed enthusiasm. Many trainers see sudden jumps in interest after a break, as if the time away helped everything settle.

A positive mindset is what carries you through long-term training. Celebrate the journey, not just the milestones. Keep a record of every win—big or small—and revisit it when your motivation dips. Slow progress is still progress. Your willingness to observe, adapt, and keep showing up matters far more than raw speed. That's what strengthens your bond and builds a thoughtful communicator. Slow and steady is how your dog builds confidence—and how you build connection.

Key Concept — Model Words Before They're Buttons

- Dogs start forming an understanding of time and availability long before they ever have buttons for those ideas.
- Use everyday language—like "later," "tomorrow," or "all gone"—whenever it naturally fits, even if the word isn't on the board yet.
- By the time you introduce a button for a concept word, your dog will already recognize the idea behind it because you've been modeling that concept all along.

REFLECTION EXERCISE: MICRO-WIN TRACKER

Each day, jot down three observations—even tiny ones—that show your dog's engagement. Did she glance at the board? Wait nearby? Hold eye contact after you modeled a word? These little notes, reviewed over time, reveal patterns of growth you might otherwise miss.

You and your dog are learning together. Some days move

quickly, others feel slow, and some feel like setbacks. This is all normal. What matters most is your presence, your observations, and your intent to nurture understanding—one press, one look, one shared moment at a time.

When things feel frustrating, pause and come back to why you began—connection, understanding, and enjoying this journey with your dog. Every step brings you closer to a meaningful conversation with your best friend.

Chapter 6

Expanding Vocabulary: Adding Words with Purpose

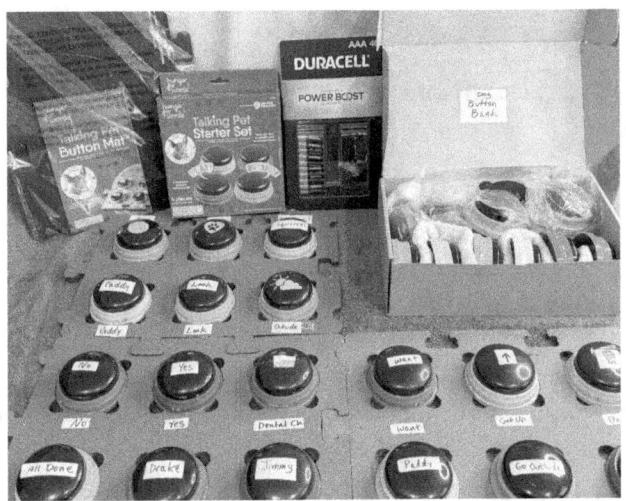

You don't need everything at once—just enough on hand to add new buttons when your dog is ready.

Choosing the Next Button—Prioritizing Needs, Context, and Dog Preferences

Expanding your dog's vocabulary isn't about copying viral videos or adding words at random. It's about providing clarity and empowering your dog to express what truly matters. Success begins with observation: What is your dog already trying to communicate nonverbally? If your dog waits by the leash after dinner, "walk" may be an ideal word to add. If he loves dropping toys in your lap, "ball" might open a new layer of joy. And if he perks up the moment the car keys jingle, "car" or "ride" may be ideal.

After observing your dog for several days, patterns start to emerge—waiting by the bed in the morning for a cuddle, or sitting by the cabinet after dinner for a treat. These aren't random behaviors; they're requests for specific words.

Creative Communication — When Dogs Think Outside the Board

I was working late when Paddy wandered in, stared at me, and slapped the "get up" button.

Thinking he was just taking the easy way out—pressing the closest button instead of stretching for the "dental chew" button—I launched into full celebration mode. I got on the floor, hauled all sixty-five pounds of him into my lap, and praised him like he'd just won gold. "Yay, Paddy! Yes! Get up! Such a smart boy!"

Then he pressed "get up" again.

So I repeated the whole routine—more cheering, more praise.

A moment later, he hit "Daddy."

"Yay, Daddy! Go find Daddy!" I encouraged.

Paddy trotted toward the front door, paused, turned back, and pressed "outside."

That's when it clicked.

Paddy didn't want attention, or a chew, or even Daddy. He wanted to go outside—and since I clearly wasn't getting up fast enough, he was escalating the conversation. If I didn't get up, he'd get Daddy to do it.

Just to make the whole thing even more impressive: those were Jimmy's buttons, not Paddy's. He had never used the "get up" button before, nor had he ever pressed "outside" at that door. But that night, he did.

(And the "get up" button was meant for Jimmy to ask to get up on the table—not for a dog to tell me to get up!)

Takeaway: Dogs don't just learn words—they learn how to use them creatively to solve problems.

Sometimes the dog really is the teacher.

Start with needs-based vocabulary—"eat," "water," "outside," "play"—but don't overlook wants. High-value words like "toy," "cuddle," and "treat" keep dogs motivated and engaged with the board.

Alternating between essentials and delights maintains both clarity and enthusiasm. "Water" might resolve confusion, while "play" keeps training fun. If your dog lights up at the sight of a squeaky toy, adding "toy" can create new shared moments. This blend of practical and enjoyable words ensures your dog can express both urgent needs and everyday joys.

Involving the whole household helps make word selection accurate and meaningful. Call a family meeting and gather observations: When does your dog act like he's trying to "say" something—through nudging, pacing, staring, or waiting? Kids may remember after-school play requests; grandparents might notice nap routines or snack cues. Create a family wishlist and rank the top five words by frequency and importance. This keeps everyone invested and ensures you don't overlook patterns.

To choose the next word, use a simple worksheet. For each potential addition, ask: How often does my dog express this desire? Can I reliably respond every time? Is the outcome immediate and rewarding? Adding "car ride," for example, may not make sense if you only drive once a month —it could lead to frustration. Prioritize words related to activities you can consistently and promptly fulfill.

INTERACTIVE WORKSHEET: NEXT WORD DECISION GUIDE

Score each item before choosing your dog's next new word.

☐ **How often does my dog express** this need or behavior?
☐ **Can I consistently follow through** when my dog uses this word?
☐ **Does this word meet a need** or bring my dog joy?
☐ **Will all household members** recognize and reinforce the word?

☐ **Will this word increase engagement** or reduce frustration?

Using this worksheet keeps your new button choices thoughtful, consistent, and grounded in real daily routines. Add up the scores. The highest-scoring word is your best next addition. Keep this worksheet handy—your dog's vocabulary grows most naturally when real life sets the pace. By observing, balancing needs and wants, and involving your household, you'll build a practical, joyful board that fits your dog's personality and enriches communication every day.

Distinguishing Similar Words—Preventing Confusion with Sound-Alike Buttons

Adding new words expands communication, but it can also create confusion if you're not deliberate about how you add them. Like us, dogs struggle when words sound too similar or have overlapping meanings. For example, your dog might press "walk" when she wants water, or "water" when she wants a walk. Introducing the buttons for "walk" and "water" at the same time can be tricky—both begin with "wa" and may be used in similar contexts. For this reason, it's best to introduce those words at different times, pairing each with other words that sound and mean something distinct.

The key is pacing. A helpful guideline is to add 2–4 new buttons every 2–4 weeks, giving your dog time to build strong associations. Don't introduce similar-sounding or related words too close together. Begin with words that differ clearly in both sound and meaning. For instance, "outside" is usually easy to learn, and once it's solid, then you can add the word "walk." Allowing time before introducing new, related words helps strong associations form and reduces confusion. Wait until your dog reliably uses the new words before introducing words with a similar meaning. When in doubt, slow the pace—taking your time now will help her learn with confidence.

Distinctiveness goes beyond sound. Use button placement and tone of voice to help your dog differentiate words. It is thought that dogs learn which buttons are which by their locations, rather than by their appearance, color, or stickers. So, although assigning them different colors—perhaps red to "toy" and blue to "ball"—may be slightly helpful at first, visual cues only minimally support memory. Avoid placing similar words next to each other at first; spacing them out allows your dog to process each one individually. When recording buttons, differentiate the tones: say "water" gently and "walk" with more energy. Over time, your dog will associate each word not only with its sound, but also with its context and mood.

Expect some confusion along the way. If your dog presses "treat" when she wants "toy," or mixes up "walk" and "water," pause and reinforce each word separately. Model the words and outcomes clearly—press "treat," say the word, then give a treat; later, do the same for "toy." Use extra enthusiasm for correct presses, keep sessions short, and maintain a low-stress environment. If confusion continues, try moving a button to a different spot on the board, but then keep it there —minor adjustments often make a big difference.

Avoid introducing look-alike or sound-alike buttons at the same time. Rapid expansion can slow learning overall and create frustration. Refer back to the list of recommended first words when choosing your subsequent additions, and add more specific or related terms only after your dog is confident using her foundational vocabulary.

Troubleshooting Checklist: When Words Are Confusing

Use this quick guide to strengthen clarity before adding more words.

☐ **Do recorded words sound too similar?**

☐ **Were related words introduced** at the same time?

☐ **Has enough practice time passed** before adding a similar-sounding or similar-meaning word?

☐ **Is your button board labeled** so buttons can be returned to the correct spots if they get moved or displaced?

Checking these points restores clarity and keeps communication frustration-free.

As your dog's vocabulary expands, you shift from teacher to guide. Notice subtle changes in button use—sometimes combinations or novel patterns arise. Stay flexible, encouraging, and observant. Every new word, introduced carefully, unlocks another part of your shared world.

Take time to set up your dog's button board. Plan ahead to put the most important buttons on one or two boards that you can take with you when you travel. Label your board as you place your buttons so they're easy to keep track of and replace if they get dislodged.

Keep a button bank for adding words every 2–4 weeks. Store extra buttons in a visible place and label them clearly with markers, stickers, or tape so people know what they say (your dog will recognize them by location and sound, as mentioned earlier). When your dog is ready, bring out your new 2–4 buttons. For some dogs, a visible button bank can spark curiosity as they explore words waiting their turn. Note: some buttons can be swapped seasonally, like "swim" in summer, "jacket" in winter.

Accessibility is important, especially in multi-pet homes or for dogs with mobility challenges. Make sure each dog can approach comfortably. You may need to encourage a bolder dog to hang back while a shy dog steps forward. (In our home, our big dog enjoys bedroom chew-bone time while our smaller dog has button training time.) For dogs with limited mobility, consider angled boards or wall-mounted setups paired with non-slip mats. Dogs missing a limb may prefer to press with their noses—try placing buttons at nose height and securing them firmly. Dogs with arthritis may need extra space between buttons to reduce slips and strain.

Thoughtful layout and accessibility ensure your dog can navigate her board comfortably, helping her learn new words with greater ease.

Introducing a new button is more than placing it out and waiting. Success comes from pairing each new word with real experiences—things your dog sees, hears, and feels. Stick to routines your dog already enjoys as your foundation.

For example, to add "play," have a toy ready. Say "play," press the button, and immediately begin playing. Press the button again and say, "We're playing!" Press it a third time and say, "Let's play!" When you're done, press once more and say, "All done play." In just one session, you've modeled the word several times, and the joy of playing reinforces the meaning.

For "water," press the button before every refill and say, "Want water?" Fill the bowl as your dog watches and say, "Here's water." Press the button again as you set the bowl down and repeat, saying "want water?" Then press the button a third time and say "water" once more. This repetition—built into a routine your dog already understands—creates a clear and reliable association.

Patience is essential—word learning develops through repetition and consistency. Remember, every dog learns new words at their own pace. If the latest word links to mealtime, use it every breakfast and dinner; for outdoor trips, use it every time you head outside. The steadier your cues, the stronger your dog's understanding becomes.

Sometimes a button remains untouched or gets pressed randomly. Don't worry—this is normal. If ignored, move it to a more visible location, or one that's easier to use, such as close to your dog's food bowl. If your dog presses it but seems unsure, increase your enthusiasm and offer extra praise for the correct use. Dogs mirror your energy. To rekindle interest, adjust timing—integrate it into a routine your dog already anticipates. Minor adjustments often reignite curiosity.

Misuse—like pressing "play" at dinner time or "water" to request outside—is common early on. Redirect gently: say the word, clarify the context ("We'll play after dinner"), and model the correct button for the current situation. Over time, your cues guide proper use.

Tracking progress helps you stay motivated and informed. Keep a simple log: note when each new word was introduced, your dog's first use (even accidental), and describe the situation. List successful presses and look for patterns: "water" after walks, "play" in the afternoon, "outside" in the morning.

Sample "New Word Log":
Word: Water
Date word introduced: April 2
First press: April 14, after breakfast
Notes: I pressed "water" before I filled it, and he looked at the bowl. He seemed interested in the button and then pressed it after I put it down!

These records become a story of shared learning.

Introducing new words through routines and scripts makes button training part of daily life rather than a separate activity. Every modeled press connects action with meaning. Each moment of patience leads to better communication. Each challenge—ignored or misused buttons—is simply another step toward deeper mutual understanding.

As your dog's vocabulary grows, progress shines in small moments of joy and recognition. Each new word builds a stronger bridge between you and your companion, making daily routines easier and more fun. In the next chapter, you'll learn how to transform single-word requests into honest conversations, letting your dog express more complex wants and ideas.

Chapter 7
Preventing and Fixing Common Problems

Jimmy spamming the buttons so fast the
camera can't keep up.

Button Spamming—Managing Overuse of Favorite Words

Imagine this: After a walk, your dog, Bee, rushes to the button board and hits "outside" again and again, hoping for another outing. You open the door once, but Bee keeps at it. This enthusiastic overuse of a favorite button is called button spamming—not disobedience, but excitement and curiosity about their new communication superpowers.

Button spamming usually happens when a dog links a button press to a reward. They may spam "outside" for extra trips, "play" for more games, or "treat" in hopes of bonus snacks. Some dogs are simply experimenting. Others are testing boundaries because persistence worked before. If spamming has been rewarded, it will continue.

The hallmark of spamming is rapid, repeated presses— like "outside" six times in minutes, sending you back and forth to the door. If your dog keeps hitting "play" after exercise or mashes "treat" until you give in, that's spamming in action. The core cause is associating the button with immediate gratification, fueled by excitement or boredom.

Managing this takes consistency—not punishment. Your rule: always acknowledge the first press positively ("Yes! Outside!") and honor the request when appropriate. If your dog circles back and presses again, pause before responding so you don't accidentally feed a spamming cycle. Ask yourself whether this is something you're okay repeating more than once in a row. Early on, that might be fine—like a second round of play when your dog is still learning the board. But as they progress, aim for a "one and done" rule: one clear press, one response. Then ignore the repeats. This teaches that one clear press works—and extras don't.

Household consistency is essential. If anyone responds to rapid-fire presses, your dog learns that persistence pays. Warmly acknowledge the first clear request, then ignore the rest. Don't scold—just withdraw attention from the extras and reinforce the single, purposeful press.

Using an "all done" signal helps mark the end of an activity. Try a hand gesture, say "all done," or cover the button briefly after granting the request. For example, after letting your dog outside, open your hands at the board and say "all done." If they press "outside" again, repeat the cue and gently redirect. For persistent spammers, temporarily cover or remove the button after the request to prevent endless loops and frustration.

As vocabulary grows, you can introduce helpful boundary-setting words like "later" or "now." If your dog spams "outside," press "later" and explain, "Outside later." Consistently model these terms, using "now" only when you mean it. It takes practice, but it helps dogs learn that not every press brings an instant reward.

Channeling extra energy also goes a long way. If spamming shows up during bored moments, offer enrichment —puzzle toys, snuffle mats, or a simple play break—to keep your dog mentally engaged. After responding to "outside," you might redirect with, "Let's play now!" and model the "play" button to shift the focus.

Button spamming comes from curiosity and opportunity. By staying consistent, setting clear boundaries, and offering engaging alternatives, you teach your dog that good communication relies on clarity—not repetition. It's the foundation of a respectful, frustration-free button dialogue.

SPAMMING SOLUTIONS CHECKLIST

Reflect on your dog's button use with these points:

☐ **Repeated Presses:** Does my dog hit the same button repeatedly within five minutes?

☐ **One-Press Response:** Do I respond only to the first press?

☐ **Clear Ending Cue:** Have I taught an "all done" sign to signal the end of activities?

☐ **Household Consistency:** Is everyone in my household responding the same way?

☐ **Enrichment Offered:** Do I offer enrichment when spamming happens?

☐ **Boundary Words Modeled:** Have I modeled "later" or "now" for repeated requests?

Consistent boundaries teach your dog that one clear request works best—and spamming doesn't speed up the process.

Multi-Pet Households—Strategies for Avoiding Cross-Talk and Interference

Training multiple pets with buttons adds complexity. Dogs may crowd the board, and cats might stroll across and trigger buttons at random. If Dog A presses "walk" while Dog B barges in—or the cat hits "treat" and excites everyone—you're seeing classic multi-pet confusion. With clear routines, each animal can participate without chaos or competition.

Minimize cross-talk by structuring training times. Stagger sessions to keep things calm. If you have two or more dogs, have one wait on a mat while the other uses the board. Colored bathmats work well as a special place for each dog to wait their turn; they're nonslip, washable, and easy for dogs to recognize by color. Teach the cue "place" so your dog knows to go to their own bathmat. For dogs who need more impulse control, keep short leashes attached to sturdy furniture for easy access; tuck them away when not in use. Most dogs quickly learn to wait patiently, which reduces tension around the board. However, if your waiting dog becomes fussy or distracting, place them in a separate room so the dog in training gets the quiet space they need to focus.

Rotating turns also helps. Try a simple system—oldest to youngest, or by favorite activities. For example, let Dog A use the board for "outside," then allow Dog B their turn—especially helpful if Dog B tends to rush in. Repeating the structure teaches fairness and patience. Some families designate separate "button time" using baby gates to curb crowding and make expectations crystal clear.

Cats, naturally curious, may nap on or stroll over the board—it's instinct, not mischief. If this disrupts training, mount the board on a low wall to discourage casual cat walk-overs while keeping it accessible for dogs. If cats persist, offer a cozy bed or a window perch nearby to draw them to a more appealing spot.

Using individual button banks can also prevent interference. Set up separate boards in different areas, personalized for each dog. This reduces competition and lets you focus on one pet at a time, though it requires more organization as each dog learns their spot. If separate boards aren't possible, help dogs understand that board access happens one at a time. Reward waiting and reinforce boundaries—especially with enthusiastic pets. Some families thrive with a shared board and turn-taking; others do better with separate setups. Choose whatever fits your household best.

Cross-talk—when one pet interrupts another's board time—calls for gentle redirection. If Dog B jumps in, calmly return them to their place and reward their patience. For persistent interrupters, move the non-participating pet to another room with an engaging toy until it's their turn. With consistency, most pets quickly adjust to the rhythm.

Observe each animal's button style. Some press with intention; others prefer a random, trial-and-error approach. Note their preferred words and any recurring confusion in your training log. If one pet routinely presses another's favorite button, give extra praise for accurate choices and gently redirect the mix-ups ("try again" or "wait"). Over time, even spirited pets learn cooperation.

Ultimately, multi-pet button training is about nurturing relationships, not just teaching vocabulary. Focus on mutual respect, clear routines, and patient guidance. With a little structure and creativity, your home can run smoothly, fairly, and peacefully—even with multiple button users.

Real Life Button Training — When Theory Meets Three Dogs and Absolute Chaos

Button training looks peaceful in videos... until you're living it with three dogs, eight new buttons, and absolutely zero regard for the recommended schedule

("2–4 buttons every 2–4 weeks"... oops—got a little behind).

You set up new buttons around the house—by the water bowl, food bowl, back door, front door, office. Then you add the newest office buttons: Drake, Jimmy, Yes, No, All Done. At the back door: Paddy, Look, Squirrel.

Paddy—your 65-lb terrier-mix manchild—marches into your office and slaps "get up." This, of course, is Jimmy's button for "want to get up on your table?", but Paddy has repurposed it into... something. You praise him anyway, haul him into your lap, and reinforce "get up" like a pro.

A few minutes later, Paddy slaps "get up" again. You ask, "Do you want me to get up?" He slaps YES. (He has had that button for four days. Four.)

You try to negotiate ("Mommy has to work"), but Paddy keeps pressing "get up" → "yes" until you finally follow him... straight to the kitchen and his food bowl. He dances around it eagerly—ignoring the perfectly placed "eat" button he used enthusiastically when it was new. Eventually, after you pretend not to know what he wants, he pounces on the button like he invented it. "AAAHHHH, Paddy—you want EAT!!!" Treats all around.

Meanwhile, Drake, your 19-lb, 15-year-old terrier-part-alligator, has decided the buttons are a mortal enemy. Every time Paddy goes near them, Drake growls, snaps, thrashes like an angry reptile, and tries to launch himself toward the board. Because he's collar-reactive, you can't redirect him easily—so you're scooping, blocking, dodging teeth, and holding him back with one hand while praising and modeling buttons with the other.

Your brain is running commentary like:

Drake stop—Paddy want?—yes—get up—no not that—Drake bed—Paddy wait—what does he want—AAARGH—

At that exact moment your husband appears in the hallway, pauses, and just... stares.

"...Do you need help?"

And you—twisted sideways, one hand fending off Drake's snapping crocodile jaws, the other hand cheerfully modeling buttons—snap without even looking at him:

"NO!

DON'T INTERRUPT!

WE'RE TRAINING."

Because yes—this is training. Messy, loud, bite-adjacent chaos... but still training.

And honestly? It counts.

Takeaway: Real communication doesn't need perfect conditions. Even in the chaos—especially in the chaos—your dog is learning.

Trainer's Note:

After this incident, I began consistently separating Drake from the buttons whenever Paddy wanted to use them. This helped keep both dogs calmer and prevented tension around the buttonboard.

Kids and Button Training—Safe, Consistent, and Fun Family Involvement

Including children in button training adds richness, but early on, the dog has no expectations at all — so consistency is the foundation on which everything builds. Kids bring energy and creativity—channel it in ways that help the dog learn. Young children need close supervision. Assign them as "button helpers": they can roll a ball after the word "ball" is pressed, or put the treat in the bowl after "eat," always with an adult guiding the flow. Adults should handle recording new words or adding buttons to maintain accuracy and expectations. Older kids can help with setup as discussed in *Chapter 2, Family Agreements*, but initial button demonstrations stay adult-led.

Consistency is vital. Families often run into trouble when members act differently, and kids may prompt dogs to press buttons out of turn. To prevent mixed signals, use unified scripts and visual cues. Place a poster above the board reading, "Say the word, press the button, then wait." This keeps everyone aligned and reinforces the wait rule, which gives dogs the time they need to process before responding. Waiting may feel awkward at first, but it prevents rushed or erratic presses. Color-coded cue cards help, too—each family member gets a card as a reminder for actions and language. Kids love having their own cards, turning consistency into part of the fun.

Kids are motivated by visible progress. Celebrate milestones with a sticker chart on the fridge, and give new words a special sticker or drawing. Kids can create a "Dog's New Word" art piece to hang near the board or add to a family gallery. These celebrations make achievements visible and build excitement. Some families hold weekly check-ins to review progress, offer rewards, or host a "Button Graduation" for significant milestones—strengthening learning and family connection.

Kids will occasionally lose interest or accidentally disrupt a session. If a child plays with buttons, laughs at the sounds, or distracts the dog, gently redirect them and remind them of their role and the wait rule. Offer alternatives: designing button labels, choosing colors, drawing word icons, or documenting training moments. Channel their energy into creative contributions instead of derailing the session. If boredom strikes, assign new roles—photographer for milestones, sticker-adder, or "family reporter" to write weekly updates for a scrapbook.

Family Button Training Toolkit

Build a "Button Training Toolkit" together. Include printed scripts ("Say the word, press the button, then wait"), color-coded cue cards, a sticker chart, art supplies for labels, and a notebook for observations—all stored in a basket in a central location or near the button board. When it's training time, everyone grabs their tool and knows their job. This routine creates excitement, keeps focus, and reinforces teamwork. If someone forgets the script, another person can offer a gentle reminder, keeping everyone on track.

Well-structured button training with kids can be both fun and effective. Assign age-appropriate duties, provide clear instructions, and celebrate together—this turns training into a family highlight. Kids build patience, the dog gains confidence, and everyone invests in the journey. The toolkit, visuals, and creative roles keep interest high and involvement meaningful. Your family becomes a unified training team, giving every member—human and canine—a voice.

When Progress Stalls — Troubleshooting Plateaus and Regression

Every button-learning dog will face setbacks. One week, your dog eagerly presses "outside" or "play," the next, the board gathers dust. A dog once fluent with "water" may stop using it or press the wrong button for familiar requests. These plateaus—periods of stalled or regressed learning—are normal. A dog might ignore the board, only respond when prompted, or mix up old words with new ones, especially after a vocabulary jump. Though discouraging, these pauses simply mean your dog is processing, reorganizing, or preparing for the next step.

Plateaus often signal readiness for progress, not failure. If your dog has mastered his current words but seems stuck, try adding two to four new ones that fit daily life —"snuggle," "car," "friend." Think about what interests your dog and watch him for clues; if he whines at you or scratches at his button board, he may be ready for a word that isn't on the board yet. Add words every 2 to 4 weeks, depending on his learning pace. Some dogs adapt quickly; others need slower changes. Observation and adaptation are key—let your training log guide your choices.

If you don't already have a training log and are considering adding one to your routine, you may find the companion journal to this book helpful: *Dog Button Training Logbook: Track Your Dog's Words, Progress, and Milestones.* It's designed to pair with *Button Training for Dogs: Teach Your Dog to Talk—A Practical Guide to Button Communication* and gives you a structured place to record vocabulary growth, patterns, and breakthroughs.

When progress halts, review your notes and look for patterns. Did the stall follow a new word? If so, does your dog seem confused? If he looks confused, temporarily remove the button—or buttons—that appear to be causing trouble. Monitor him and record whether he returns to his usual button behavior. If he does, leave the problematic buttons off for a while and introduce different ones instead. On the other hand, if boredom seems likely, add a few new buttons. This boosts interest by giving him more choices and opportunities for engagement.

Sometimes a change in environment or timing reignites motivation. If the board has always been in the kitchen, move it to the living room or near a favorite window—new locations spark curiosity. Adjust session timing—after a walk, before breakfast, or whenever your dog is most alert. Even changing the mat or board texture can prompt renewed engagement.

During plateaus, avoid focusing on what isn't happening. Celebrate small successes. If your dog sniffs the board after ignoring it for days, that counts. If he looks at you after hearing a familiar word, that's progress. Set tiny, achievable goals: one press or one approach per day. When he meets those goals, reward him with praise, a happy tone, or some playtime. Treat the first successful press after downtime as a big event. Recalibrate your expectations—progress is measured in effort and reconnection, not word count.

If you feel frustrated, remember: plateaus and setbacks are part of learning—for both dogs and humans. These moments offer a chance to observe and adjust. Maybe your dog needs a new challenge, a break in routine, or extra patience while he consolidates skills. Stay flexible. Log each change and keep your focus on progress, not perfection.

In closing, see setbacks as a natural part of communication. When you approach plateaus with patience, creativity, and adaptability, you pave the way for growth. The next chapter will guide you in expanding your dog's vocabulary and deepening your shared conversations, turning small wins into lasting progress.

Chapter 8
Personalizing Training for Every Dog

Jimmy as a half-grown puppy, full of curiosity
and eager to learn.

Button Training with Puppies—Setting Up for Lifelong Communication

Puppies brim with energy and curiosity—making early puppyhood an ideal window for learning. This is the perfect time to introduce button training, helping young dogs grasp not only core routines but also the basics of "talking" about their needs. Early exposure to communication tools does more than teach—it builds trust, curiosity, and a natural interest in exploring how things work.

Between eight and sixteen weeks, puppies' brains are highly receptive, absorbing surroundings quickly. Introducing buttons during this phase helps form lifelong associations. When you press the "outside" button before heading out or the "play" button before fun, your puppy begins to link those cues with real-world activities. Communication becomes as familiar as any household sound.

Pair button training with early socialization. Make button sounds just another new experience, introduced gently, the same way you would new environments, surfaces, or objects. Play recordings softly and pair each sound with warmth, praise, or playful interaction. The goal is for button sounds to become as routine and positive as toys or water bowls. Ask yourself: Does your puppy hear button sounds daily? Are presses consistently linked with meaningful actions? Are words like "water" and "play" modeled during real moments? A simple checklist helps ensure buttons become a seamless part of her early world.

Remember that puppies have extremely short attention spans—often just seconds. Long sessions lead to frustration. Keep training light and playful: two to three minutes at a time, woven into natural parts of the day. Use movement to keep her engaged: press "play," then toss a ball; press "outside," then walk together to the door. Try a simple game like "Find the 'Play' Button" by hiding the board under a toy or small blanket. If your puppy presses a button —even accidentally—acknowledge it with excitement and interaction. Focus on curiosity and engagement, not precision.

Begin with "play": press the button, bring out the toy, and engage her in a short game while you model the word several times. Repeat until she naturally winds down for a nap. After some play, model "outside," then take her out to potty. When you come back in, model "water" and offer a drink. Then enjoy a little more play. Before she rests again, model "bed" as you guide her to her spot. If her first four words are "play," "outside," "water," and "bed," you'll have plenty of natural opportunities to model all four several times a day.

For structure, place the button board on a brightly colored mat to signal "communication time." Over time, she'll associate the mat with fun learning. Celebrate every small sign of progress—prioritizing positive associations over perfect accuracy.

Even though you'll be busy with your puppy, try to keep a simple log of sessions, words used, moments of interest, and accidental presses. Patterns become easier to spot when you document them, helping you adjust training as your puppy grows.

Puppies are notorious chewers, and some may gnaw on buttons. Limit access to supervised sessions and put the board away between trainings. If she starts chewing, calmly offer a chew toy instead. No scolding is needed—she'll soon learn that buttons are for paws (or noses) and toys are for chewing.

Puppy learning pace varies—some press buttons within days, others take weeks. What matters is keeping it fun, pressure-free, and woven into real life. Early button exposure helps communication become second nature, setting your puppy up for lifelong understanding and success—not just with buttons, but with every form of communication.

EARLY PUPPY LEARNING CHECKLIST

Use this quick checklist to help your puppy build early, positive associations with button sounds and everyday routines.

☐ **Daily Sound Exposure:** Does your puppy hear each button sound at least twice a day?

☐ **Meaningful Pairing:** Are presses paired with praise, play, or meaningful actions?

☐ **Short Sessions:** Are sessions kept short (2–3 minutes) and fun?

☐ **Consistent Logging:** Are you keeping a simple, consistent log of your puppy's button use?

If you answered mostly "yes," you're building a solid foundation for long-term communication.

Adapting for Senior Dogs—Gentle Techniques and Accessibility Tools

Senior dogs bring wisdom, but their bodies and minds may be slowing. You might notice hesitation stepping up, slower movement, or favoring one side. Stiff joints and age-related aches can make bending for buttons uncomfortable.

Reluctance to lie down, sit, or rise again may be subtle clues. When introducing button training, adapt for comfort and accessibility. If your dog hesitates or misses the button, consider discomfort—not disinterest. Memory lapses are normal with age and may cause slower responses or temporary forgetfulness. These moments call for patience and flexibility.

Author's Note—Drake's Story

My own senior dog, Drake, reminds me daily how much older dogs still want to participate, even if the world moves a bit too fast around them. Years ago, he learned to touch-mark a target stick with his nose—he and our little Pomeranian, Bhalu, mastered it together. So when Drake grew older and frailer, I thought I could transfer that behavior to button pressing. And he got it immediately—he's no dummy.

But Drake has always been a gentle soul. His touches are feather-light, more like a whisper than a press. He understands the goal, he targets the button beautifully... but he often doesn't press quite hard enough to make it "talk." Add two boisterous, bigger dogs bouncing around nearby, and it becomes even harder for him to get his turn.

So we go slowly. Some days he tries. Some days he watches. Some days we practice touching the button softly, without asking for more. It's an ongoing project—one we'll keep working on together, at his pace. Senior dogs don't need to meet a timeline; they need to feel included, respected, and heard.

Drake pressing a button with his nose.

Make button use easier by adjusting the setup. If pressing seems difficult, don't worry—most dog buttons aren't adjustable. Instead, make simple modifications to help your senior succeed: raise the board a few inches, angle it slightly, or place it at nose height so she can nudge it comfortably. Add non-slip backing or small Velcro squares to keep the buttons from sliding, and position them near her favorite resting area to reduce extra walking. Keep pathways clear, minimize clutter, and use contrasting colors to help with aging vision. If she prefers nudging with her nose instead of using her paw, embrace that—let her choose what feels comfortable.

For seniors, keep training short, frequent, and low-key. Early afternoons—after rest and when stiffness has eased—often work best. Minimize background noise and distractions to help her focus. When you model a button, pause longer than you would with a younger dog; give her time to process. Avoid repeating words too quickly or adding urgency. Seniors thrive with gentle repetition and slower pacing. Five or six calm, unhurried minutes often work far better for seniors than the quick, high-energy sessions a young dog might enjoy.

Progress is worth celebrating, no matter how small. Pressing "water" for the first time in weeks or remembering "outside" after a lapse are bright victories. Try using a simple visual tracker—create a "Senior Success Stories" board and add stickers or notes for each step: "First Press at 12 Years," "Remembered 'Cuddle' Today." Invite the household to join in—take photos, write quick notes, and celebrate together. Daily reflection on her communication—even a hopeful nudge rather than a full press—keeps the focus on connection, not perfection.

If you have more than one dog, ensure enthusiastic younger companions don't crowd out your senior. Guide her to the board and let her practice without pressure. If needed, briefly separate the dogs so she can have quiet time to engage at her own pace. Watch for signs that she's tired or ready for a break; honoring those cues maintains her confidence and comfort. The goal isn't to compare her progress to younger dogs, but to respect her rhythm.

Aging dogs move through the world at their own pace. Your senior may take longer, but the communication you build together is meaningful. By adjusting the environment, slowing the process, and celebrating each win, you're supporting her voice and strengthening your bond. With patience and thoughtful accommodations, your senior can continue expressing needs and emotions for years to come.

SENIOR DOG COMFORT & COMMUNICATION CHECKLIST

Use this checklist to ensure your senior dog's communication setup supports comfort, mobility, and confidence.

☐ **Are the buttons placed** near your dog's favorite resting spot?

☐ **Is the board raised, angled, or mounted** at a height that's easy for nose nudges?

☐ **Do the buttons stay stable** with non-slip backing or Velcro?

☐ **Are pathways to the board clear** and uncluttered?

☐ **Do you allow extra time** after modeling a word before expecting a response?

☐ **Are training sessions short,** calm, and free from distractions?

☐ **Is your senior getting quiet practice time** without younger dogs crowding in?

☐ **Are you celebrating small wins and noting** moments of interest or effort?

These small considerations help your senior dog stay comfortable, confident, and willing to keep communicating with you.

Veterinarian's Voice: Supporting Comfort and Health in Senior Dogs

As a veterinarian, I always encourage owners of senior dogs to look at mobility first. If your older dog hesitates at the button board, misses presses, or seems reluctant to shift her weight, it may not be a training issue at all—it may be discomfort. Back pain, knee arthritis, and hip arthritis/dysplasia are extremely common in aging dogs.

If your senior hasn't had a mobility check recently, this is a good time to have your veterinarian evaluate her for pain.

There are many ways we can help. Joint supplements such as glucosamine and chondroitin can support comfort, and medications like Adequan or other prescription therapies may significantly improve ease of movement. Even small improvements in comfort often translate into greater confidence, ability to move freely, and willingness to use the buttons.

In my animal chiropractic practice, I frequently see senior dogs regain fluidity, balance, and overall quality of life with gentle chiropractic adjustments. When a dog feels aligned and more comfortable in her body, she's more able—and more willing—to engage with her environment, including her communication board.

Another important point: if your dog hasn't had recent lab work, including a urine test, now is a good time to check in with your veterinarian. Kidney issues and urinary tract infections are surprisingly common in older dogs. These serious conditions often go undetected and can cause discomfort, restlessness, or reluctance to approach the board. A simple urine test every 6–12 months can catch problems early and relieve a great deal of discomfort once addressed.

Button hesitation in seniors is often a message—not of confusion, but of physical needs. By supporting joint health, managing pain, and monitoring internal wellness, you help your senior dog stay comfortable, confident, and able to keep "talking" with you in the ways that matter most.

🐾 🐾

Special Needs Solutions—Vision, Hearing, and Mobility Adaptations

For dogs with vision loss, every sensory cue matters. Without full sight, tactile details become essential. Add textures to the buttons—Velcro, felt, ribbed fabric, or small patches of faux fur—to help your dog distinguish each word by touch as well as by its location and sound. "Water" might be fuzzy, "outside" ribbed, "cuddle" soft. Keep the board in a consistent location, since that predictability is the most important thing for a visually impaired dog.

Guide your dog's paw or nose gently toward each button, naming the texture and the word together to help her explore confidently. This is the one exception to the general rule of never placing your dog's paw on the buttons with your hands—dogs with significant vision loss often need this brief tactile guidance to orient themselves and make sense of the board.

For daily safety and confidence, I strongly recommend a halo-style device designed for blind dogs, such as **Muffin's Halo – The Original Blind Dog Halo.** Halos protect a dog's head from bumping into furniture, bushes, and other obstacles in their path. If your dog wears a halo, you may need to remove it during button sessions so she can touch the buttons with her nose freely.

Sound can also be a valuable cue for blind or partially sighted dogs. Record different voices for different words—a lower tone for "food," a higher pitch for "play," even a cheerful laugh for "cuddle." Blind dogs quickly learn to follow these unique auditory signatures. Attaching a small chime or bell near the board can help your dog orient herself. For dogs who are both blind and deaf, tactile variety, consistent placement, and predictable routines become the primary tools for successful communication.

For partially sighted, blind, or blind-and-deaf dogs, light and vibration cues can also support communication. If your dog responds well to vibration, place the board on a rubber mat on a non-carpeted floor. Then tap your foot or hand near the board to create a gentle vibration your dog can feel through her paws. This can help blind-and-deaf dogs locate you and orient toward the communication area. Flicking a light, waving your hand, or making another visible motion can also help signal dogs who still notice visual changes.

Deaf or hard-of-hearing dogs rely heavily on visual cues. Pair modeled button presses with precise, familiar gestures— point to the toy basket when you press "play," walk toward the door as you press "outside." If your dog already knows some basic obedience hand signals, expand their meaning: a thumbs-up for "yes," a wave for "come," a flat palm for "wait." I recommend using basic American Sign Language signs when teaching visual cues. ASL keeps your family's signals consistent, and it allows anyone familiar with it to communicate easily with your dog. Keep gestures crisp, consistent, and clear enough for your dog to see easily.

Mobility limitations call for thoughtful modifications. Dogs using wheelchairs, dogs with three legs, or dogs with arthritis may find bending or shifting weight difficult. Mounting buttons at nose height along a stable wall can dramatically increase accessibility. Choose soft-touch or oversized buttons if available—anything that allows a light nudge to activate the sound. Angling the board forward or elevating it a few inches helps dogs who can't reach the floor comfortably.

For dogs with missing limbs, experiment with placement, angle, and button spacing until you find what works best for their body. For dogs with muscle weakness or mobility issues, lowering the board or widening the spacing between buttons may make communication easier and more comfortable.

Above all, stay flexible. Watch how your dog approaches the board and make minor adjustments as needed. If she tires easily, shorten sessions or move the board to a more convenient spot. Allow plenty of time for exploration—there's no need to rush. Every sniff, pause, and attempt is meaningful. Adaptation is as much a mindset as mechanics, and celebrating your dog's creative problem-solving keeps communication joyful, accessible, and worthwhile.

Visual Exercise: Sensory Mapping for Button Boards

Create a simple sketch of your dog's button board. Mark where each button is located and note the texture you added to it—dots for Velcro, lines for ribbed fabric, stars for felt, or whatever symbols make sense to your family. Add the hand signal or gesture that matches each word. Post this "sensory map" where everyone can see it. It becomes a shared guide, helping your whole family stay consistent and support your dog's abilities.

Adaptation makes button training possible for every dog, regardless of challenge. Build language around your dog's senses, strengths, and unique ways of interacting with the world; make communication accessible for all.

Breed-Specific Strategies—Recognizing and Leveraging Instincts

Breed instincts shape how each dog learns, plays, and communicates. Button training works best when it aligns with what your dog naturally loves to do.

Herding Breeds

Border Collies, Australian Shepherds, and Corgis thrive on staying busy and problem-solving. Buttons like "job," "herd," or "help" give structure to their day. Build sessions around tasks: after pressing "job," have your dog "help" carry laundry, gather toys, or follow directional cues. Use puzzle toys or introduce new buttons a little sooner than average to keep their quick minds engaged without overwhelming them.

Retrievers

Labradors and Golden Retrievers shine with fetch, carry, and social play. Buttons like "ball," "fetch," and "bring" fit their instincts perfectly. Press "ball," toss the toy, and celebrate their retrieve like it's championship-level work. They learn best in short bursts between play.

Scent Hounds

These hounds naturally lead with their noses, but button work doesn't need to become a scent-tracking challenge. Keep it simple. Place your dog's favorite toy in plain sight—just a foot away—press "find," and let her locate it with her nose (or her eyes, if she prefers). This gives hounds a chance to be successful at what they're instinctively wired to do. If she's feeling more energetic, move the toy slightly farther away, but it never needs to be a complicated hunt. Calm scenting activities suit many hounds—yes, even the occasional wild Beagle—and help channel that instinct into an activity she can readily succeed at and thoroughly enjoy.

Guarding and Working Breeds

German Shepherds, Doberman Pinschers, and Rottweilers appreciate clarity and structure. Buttons like "watch," "friend," or "check" allow them to express awareness. Introduce words slowly and keep routines consistent—these thoughtful dogs thrive on reliable expectations.

Body Shape and Size

Dachshunds and French Bulldogs may need low or angled buttons, while Great Danes prefer boards mounted at nose-height. Enthusiastic pressers may benefit from boards secured with Velcro, set on rubber mats, or weighted.

Mixed Breeds

Mixed-breed and rescue dogs blend instincts in surprising ways. Let their preferences guide you—a dog with herding and retrieving tendencies might develop unique "dialects," like pressing "window" before birdwatching. Stay flexible.

Vocabulary should match your dog's natural motivators. Observe which words spark excitement and which ones she ignores, and adjust accordingly.

Above all, respect your dog's background and strengths. Button training is more than vocabulary; it's building bridges between instinct, curiosity, and individuality.

Chapter 9
Keeping It Fresh: Maintaining Momentum and Avoiding Burnout

A younger Paddy, ready for some ball play.

Preventing Button Fatigue—Signs, Solutions, and Session Scheduling

Remember the thrill of your dog's very first button press— maybe you felt awe, pride, or that spark of "we're really doing this." Over time, though, that initial rush can mellow. Your dog may wander off, seem less enthusiastic, or approach the board half-heartedly. You might find yourself checking the clock, repeating the same cues, or feeling a little drained. Motivation naturally ebbs and flows for both humans and dogs. Recognizing early signs of fatigue helps keep communication joyful rather than dutiful.

If your dog knows the word but won't press the button— he wants the thing itself—don't take it personally. I went through something similar when teaching my two-year-old son ASL. He wasn't hearing impaired—we simply wanted to give him an easier way to communicate before he really started talking. He picked up dozens of signs and became wonderfully expressive. Then along came our daughter. That little stinker just wanted what she wanted. Minimal signing, minimal interest—she'd skip the communication piece entirely and head straight for the thing she desired. Was she stubborn? I think so. And some dogs do the same.

When this happens, return to what worked in the beginning: model with your cheerful, upbeat voice, and don't pressure your dog to participate. Keep demonstrating words naturally and ignore their level of engagement for now. Sometimes this "stubbornness" is really a sign of boredom. Your dog may be ready for something new, and introducing two to four fresh words can re-energize their interest. (Refer to Chapter 4 for adding new vocabulary and Chapter 8 for more troubleshooting tips.)

Button fatigue can creep in quietly. In dogs, look for small shifts: approaching the board reluctantly, giving only a quick sniff, yawning, pausing before responding, sighing, or walking away mid-session. Some simply settle onto their beds and turn their heads away from the board. On your side, signals include boredom, irritability, distraction, or rising impatience. If you catch yourself checking your phone, raising your voice, or feeling frustrated with slow progress, that's your cue to adjust your pace.

Pacing is essential. Short sessions—just three to six minutes—are plenty for many dogs and handlers. Keep your goals small: one or two words per session is enough. Don't expect perfect presses every time. Instead, let each session unfold naturally. Rotate the focus you give and the reward you use. Sometimes praise is the reward. Other times, a little play, a short tug game, or going outside is all the motivation your dog needs. Vary your reinforcers to keep training enjoyable and free of pressure for both of you.

A relaxed environment matters. If your dog hesitates or falters, stay patient. Dogs read our tone, posture, and even our breathing. If you feel your stress rising, pause. Step away for a moment, stretch, breathe, or give your dog a break, too. Training should always feel like a shared adventure—not a chore to check off.

A flexible schedule is your best defense against burnout. Avoid rigid "training blocks" that feel like appointments. Instead, weave button practice naturally into daily life—before breakfast, after a walk, or while watching TV. Try setting up your week to include focused sessions, casual button use, and at least one real day off. For example:

- **Monday, Wednesday, Friday:** short, focused sessions
- **Tuesday or Saturday:** an additional no-practice or minimal-practice day
- **Thursday:** casual button use during play or walks
- **Sunday:** an actual rest day

Even on minimal-practice days, continue modeling naturally so your dog doesn't go too long without hearing their words.

This rhythm keeps both you and your dog engaged without feeling chained to structure. If your family is involved, check in regularly. A brief monthly conversation—"What's working? What feels tiring? Should we swap roles?"—keeps everyone aligned and prevents resentment or boredom. Adjust session times to match everyone's natural energy peaks. Some dogs (and people) shine in the morning; others focus better in the evening. Flexibility preserves enthusiasm and engagement.

Preventing burnout isn't about pushing harder. It's about tuning in—to your dog's body language, your own emotions, and the shifting rhythms of daily life. Progress often emerges during relaxed, pressure-free moments. By staying honest, flexible, and gentle with yourselves, you create a sustainable path toward rich, meaningful communication as you continue forward together.

Sustained motivation hinges on variety, and rotating words, games, and activities is an easy way to keep things fresh. If your dog fixates on the same words or seems bored by the board, refresh the setup. Swap little-used buttons for timely, seasonal options. In autumn, introduce "pumpkin," paired with showing your dog a toy pumpkin, a real pumpkin from the store, or—if you want to stretch the rules a bit—a tiny lick of canned pumpkin. In summer, add a "beachball" button for outdoor play. Rotating themed words sparks curiosity and undeniably makes sessions more fun. Sprinkle in special-event vocabulary—"fireworks" in July or "birthday" for celebrations. These small changes revive your dog's interest and keep communication relevant.

REFLECTION EXERCISE CHECKLIST: BUTTON FATIGUE SELF-CHECK

Use these questions to guide your weekly adjustments:
- ☐ **My dog is engaged** and not avoiding the board
- ☐ **I feel calm and interested** during training
- ☐ **We had at least one "button-free" day** this week
- ☐ **I used varied rewards** — praise, play, or activities
- ☐ **All sessions stayed under ten minutes**
- ☐ **I checked in with my family** about what's working
- ☐ **Sessions matched our natural high-energy times**

If even one answer is "no," adjust your pace this week — more rest, shorter sessions, or a small routine shift.

When Your Dog Misses the Swapped Button

If you rotate a button out, stay alert for signs your dog may want it back. She might paw at the empty spot, whine, pace, or stand at the former button location without pressing anything.

These subtle cues often mean she's looking for the swapped button to communicate something familiar or important. If you notice this, simply put the original button back and observe her response.

Add social variety whenever you can. Dogs often respond to novelty in *people* just as much as novelty in words. If training always involves the same person, motivation can dip. Invite a friend or neighbor your dog knows well to run a short session or prompt different words—a new person's enthusiasm can reignite your dog's engagement and interest. In families, keep it simple and take turns: one person prompts, another praises, and another records a few notes or observes. Even small shifts in who participates can bring fresh energy, helping your dog stay engaged.

Make sessions playful. Game-based training enlivens the board and exercises both body and mind. Try a simple "hide-and-seek" game: place a well-known button that's easy to reward—like "ball"—in a new spot, such as behind a chair or under a table, and encourage your dog to find and press it. Then have a fun celebration together. This taps into natural problem-solving instincts and offers a light challenge with an immediate, satisfying reward through play and your shared excitement.

Another fun game, once she knows several words, is "Simon Says." Prompt her to press the called-out words and cheer when she gets it right. For a twist, let her press a button ("play," "cuddle," or "walk") and you follow her lead. Of course, each press gets a big party—your enthusiasm is the reward that keeps the game lively and fun.

Break reward monotony. Predictable responses can dull enthusiasm. Some days, reward a correct press with energetic play; on others, offer a long cuddle, a joyful greeting, or a favorite game. If the button is "cuddle," give an uninterrupted snuggle. For "play," vary the activity: tug one day, a quick chase the next. Varying the style of these non-food rewards reinvigorates learning and reveals whether your dog prioritizes toys, touch, movement, or social connection. Let observations steer your response. Your log is one of your best tools here; looking back will help you spot what motivates your dog, which rewards land well, and what needs refreshing.

Create "themed weeks" to introduce structure and new vocabulary. Try "Adventure Week" ("car," "park," "trail") or "Cozy Week" ("blanket," "nap," "video"). Rotate buttons based on your dog's evolving interests; retire "squeaky" if it's stale, and spotlight "pool" as the weather shifts outdoors.

Refreshing the routine doesn't need to be complex. Simply rearranging buttons or swapping two can reignite curiosity. Stay responsive to your dog's mood. Notice hesitation or boredom? Switch up words, invent a game, or change with the seasons. Flexibility keeps communication engaging, lively, and central to your bond.

Celebrating Micro-Wins—The Power of Progress Trackers and Badges

Each new button press—especially in a new context—is meaningful. Maybe your dog used "outside" at a friend's home, or confidently pressed "water" when the bathroom bowl was empty rather than the kitchen bowl. These steps, however subtle, build the foundation for your shared language. Noticing and celebrating these micro-achievements invigorates motivation. For your dog, every smile or cheer affirms her willingness to persist.

Progress tracking transforms hidden growth into a

daily celebration. Focus on incremental victories—pressing a word unprompted, responding in a novel setting, or maintaining eye contact before pressing. Magnetized charts, such as the *Hunger for Words Talking Pet Goal Tracker*, offer a visible way for all household members to spot advancement. Kids love moving magnets as words are mastered, while adults appreciate seeing tangible progress. Journaling in resources like the *Teach Your Dog to Talk* companion log provides space to record observations, detail breakthroughs, and identify emerging patterns; it's also ideal for noting "firsts," such as using new words or resuming after a break. **For printable trackers, badges, and an expanding collection of downloadable resources, visit kmuellerpublishing.com.**

Badges reward specific milestones. Printable or crafted badges—bright and customized—celebrate progress: "Bravery Badge" for conquering button shyness, "Helper Badge" for a participant's involvement, or "Persistence Badge" for repeated attempts. Badges structure the process and make achievements visible, whether displayed on a fridge, bulletin board, or family notebook. Unique magnets or stickers can highlight achievements tailored to your dog, like "First Press with Grandma Watching" or "Inventing a Combo."

Celebrations foster accountability and fuel motivation. Capture badge moments in photos or videos, share logbook entries with friends, or post progress updates in support forums. Private recognition works too—a changing fridge display keeps everyone mindful of current achievements. These celebrations reinforce ongoing engagement and often inspire renewed excitement, especially when external encouragement is provided.

Ultimately, celebrating micro-wins creates partnership.

Rather than fixating on distant targets or comparison, you'll learn to appreciate subtle progress—using familiar words in unexpected settings, pressing with confidence, or simply paying closer attention. These shifts testify to deepening communication and mutual trust. By recognizing and celebrating small steps, training becomes less about goals and more about building joyful, shared experiences.

INTERACTIVE ELEMENT: MICRO-WIN BADGE MAKER

Start a home badge system. Design or print badges for milestones like "First Press in a New Place," "Most Creative Combo," or "Family Helper of the Week." Let family members select which to pursue next and decide together how to showcase them—on the fridge, in a scrapbook, or using digital stickers. This creative process makes daily progress visible and memorable for all.

When to Take a Break—Recognizing and Respecting Your Dog's Limits

Recognizing when to pause button training is as crucial as mastering new words. Notice your dog's mood and subtle signals, such as lingering yawns, turning away, or a drooping tail. More pronounced indicators include walking away mid-session, disengaging, or spamming buttons as if to hasten the lesson's end. Such cues reflect mental or physical overload—not disobedience or lack of ability. Watch for signs like licking, stress-panting, or distraction by itches; these are requests for a break. Forcing learning in these moments only erodes confidence and joy.

Breaks are not setbacks, but wise and necessary. They allow your dog's mind to process, much like letting a stew simmer rather than constantly stirring. After a breakthrough, such as mastering a new word, schedule a "button vacation" to help information integrate. During busy stretches—holidays, visitors, travel—release the pressure by pausing structured training entirely. Let your dog enjoy the change; you can always pick up again later, often with renewed enthusiasm.

Genuine breaks shift focus from formal training to pure enrichment. Use button-free days for relaxing "sniff" walks, rotating favorite toys, or offering puzzle feeders for novel stimulation. Cuddle time or quiet backyard moments restore energy, deepen connection, and take away any sense of pressure. These restful activities mean your dog often returns to the buttons refreshed, with fewer random presses and more enthusiasm

When resuming training, keep it simple and positive. Start with one or two well-liked words—such as "outside" or a playful button like "ball." Shower praise for any interaction: if your dog glances at, sniffs, or nudges a button, consider it a win. You might reward your dog with her very favorite thing—a special chew, a new toy, or her favorite puzzle—as a joyful way to return to button time. This can erase any residual stress and reinforce that the board is for pleasure, not pressure.

Anticipate temporary rustiness after breaks. Your dog might seem hesitant at first—it's perfectly normal. Go slowly, celebrating any attempt. Growth isn't a race; partnership is the focus. Gentle encouragement, patience, and play bring back skills swiftly and encourage new growth.

Remember, taking breaks is not failure but essential to the learning process. Both of you need time for rest, reflection, and enjoyment. Responding to your dog's need for breaks demonstrates respect and sustains trust. The aim isn't flawless performance, but a communication partnership—built one press and one response at a time.

Big picture, learning your dog's needs for rest helps keep training enjoyable and sustainable. Meeting these moments with compassion and flexibility not only strengthens your bond but also makes each new success all the more meaningful. Next, you'll learn how to move beyond single words to initiate richer, more nuanced conversations.

Signs Your Dog Needs a Break

Watch for these subtle cues that you might need to pause training and reset:
- **yawning** or repeated yawns
- **turning away** from you or the board
- **lowered posture** or a drooping tail
- **licking or stress-panting**
- **sudden distraction** or "busy" behavior
- **disengaging** or spamming buttons

If you notice any of these cues, pause the session. A quick pause in the right moment helps keep training joyful and frustration-free.

Chapter 10
Combining Buttons: Teaching
Short Phrases and Sequencing

Paddy independently pressing buttons.

Watching my own dog, Paddy, move from single-button presses to combining words was a transformative moment. One evening, he came into my office and pressed "get up, outside"—two clear, consecutive presses, directed unmistakably at me. He did it again a few days later with the same sequence, the same intention, and the same expectant look. These simple two-word combinations showed how dogs naturally begin linking ideas when they're ready, and how sequencing allows them to express specific needs with clarity.

Teach sequences by modeling button combinations within context. When your dog shows interest in playing, say the phrase—such as "want play"—and press "want," then "play." Immediately follow through by starting the game. Consistent modeling during daily routines pairs each word sequence with its outcome. Through repetition and observation, your dog begins to understand that pressing words in order carries meaning. Sequencing takes time, so keep sessions short and positive.

After a modeling period, your dog may start pressing one or both buttons alone. If he presses only "want" or only "play," acknowledge the effort, then gently model the complete phrase and respond to it. Gradually reduce assistance as he becomes more confident in combining buttons independently. Even with pauses between presses, treat it as intentional progress—sequencing is about meaning, not speed.

Dogs process some things more slowly than we do. When it comes to using word buttons, they often need a moment—sometimes several—to think. Putting words together requires concentration and processing time, so let them take the time it takes. Put your human schedule on pause and give your dog 1 to 2 minutes of quiet thinking time. Some dogs need even more, especially when trying to combine several words.

If you watch Bunny or other dogs on social media, you may notice the camera occasionally skips ahead to allow for "thinking time." Even Bunny, who is highly accomplished with her buttons, needs significant time to organize and express her thoughts. It's a beautiful process—let it unfold.

Expect challenges like "button mashing." Some dogs press multiple buttons rapidly, hoping something will work. Break the sequence down, reinforce each word individually until he's pressing deliberately, then model the whole combination slowly. A "pause and prompt" method—pausing after the first button, then indicating the next—helps encourage thoughtful presses rather than frantic ones.

If he repeatedly presses only one button from the sequence, strengthen each word individually before reintroducing combinations. Some dogs benefit from visual or tactile guidance, such as pointing to the next button or lightly tapping the board. Clear, consistent feedback helps him understand when he's making correct attempts and when to try again.

As sequencing comes together, your dog's requests become more specific and easier to interpret. Moving from single-button use to meaningful two-word phrases is a significant communication milestone—one that turns everyday interactions into richer, more collaborative conversations.

INTERACTIVE EXERCISE: PHRASE-BUILDING PROGRESS CHART

Set up a chart with three columns: Date, Phrase Modeled ("want play," "want outside"), and Dog's Attempt (single, partial, or complete sequence). Record what you modeled and how your dog responded—note out-of-order presses, pauses, or breakthroughs. Tracking progress makes his journey from single words to clear combinations visible and encouraging.

Contextual Use—Helping Your Dog Generalize Words Across Situations

Early in button training, dogs often associate a word with its training spot. Your dog might press "outside" only near the back door and ignore it elsewhere. This reliance on patterns is normal, but richer communication comes when he generalizes —realizing that "outside" means the same thing anywhere, or that "park" refers to the same concept—a walk or play area— across different settings. Without this step, his vocabulary stays local, tied to specific situations instead of ideas.

Encourage generalization through deliberate, playful practice. Move a familiar button—like "water"—to new spots such as the living room or backyard. When he presses it, immediately praise him and meet the request; this teaches him that words travel with him. Try shifting the location of your button board—slightly at first—and watch to be sure it doesn't unsettle your dog. If he's comfortable with a small change, move it to another room and see how he does with generalizing his buttons. If you haven't already, you can also involve family or friends as responders, showing him that communication works with more than just you.

A portable button board allows real-world generalization. Create a small travel kit with essentials such as "water," "potty," and "home," and use it during walks, errands, or visits. Always respond to his button presses regardless of where you are. If he asks for "water" at a café, provide it; if he asks for "potty" at a relative's house, take him out. These experiences demonstrate that his words have meaning everywhere.

True generalization emerges when your dog uses buttons naturally in new places. He might press "outside" at the front door after only using it at the back, or request "play" at a friend's home. Each time he uses a button outside its original context—and receives the expected result—he's showing a deepening understanding of each word's meaning and growing communication flexibility.

Monitor for progress cues that reveal expanding understanding. Notice when he searches for a relocated button, presses it after it's moved, or communicates successfully with someone new. A simple progress log can help: jot down examples like, "Pressed 'water' in backyard," or "Used 'outside' with neighbor." Over time, these small notes reveal how his confidence and versatility are growing.

Support this growth with patience and encouragement. Some dogs linger in early routines or find new locations overwhelming. If he struggles, model the word several times in the new space before expecting independent use. Praise every communication attempt—including ones that follow your prompting. Keeping sessions positive and varied helps him generalize more quickly.

REFLECTION SECTION: WHERE DID MY DOG USE IT?

At week's end, review all the places and situations where each button was used, noting when he acted independently versus after assistance. Did he press "water" somewhere new? Did he use "play" with someone else? Use your log to highlight progress and identify words that need more practice. Generalization isn't just a training milestone—it's evidence that your dog is learning to communicate wherever he finds himself.

Reading Intent—How to Tell When Your Dog Really Means It

With more vocabulary, reading your dog's intent becomes subtler—and far more fulfilling. Early on, button presses can appear random, but as his skills develop, patterns of genuine communication emerge. Spotting intentional presses involves paying attention to timing, body language, consistency, and context.

Observe him before and after he presses a button. True requests are typically paired with signals: he may look at you, then at the door before pressing "outside," or pace and whine before "help." Dogs communicating intentionally often make eye contact, alternate their gaze between you and the board, and wait for your reaction. A focused or alert posture—ears forward, still tail—suggests expectation. At other times, he may walk straight to the board and press a button with quiet confidence, clearly knowing what he wants to say without pausing to look around. Reacting appropriately—such as pressing "treat" when the jar rattles or "play" when you pick up a toy—reflects a solid understanding of the word and its meaning.

Consistency is another strong indicator. If he presses "eat" before every meal or "potty" at regular times, he has learned to connect the words on the buttons to his daily needs. When Paddy learned "eat," he began pressing it at every meal—and occasionally during our mealtimes, too. We responded with, "Yes, we eat. We're eating dinner now. Your eat is later—you eat dinner later." We were thrilled he was using the word, and we always acknowledged the press, using our words to help him understand the concept of later and to gently expand his vocabulary. Over time, as he learned the difference between "eat" for himself and humans eating, he began using the button with better timing.

Intent appears most clearly when a button is used repeatedly in a predictable context. Pressing "outside" each morning, for example, or consistently requesting "play" after dinner shows purposeful communication. Look for eye contact, pressing "outside," then waiting by the door, or pressing "eat," then standing by the food bowl. Additional cues—nudging the button, whining, pacing, or pressing again if you don't respond—can show his intent.

Track communication with a simple checklist. Does he press a button three times in the same context? Does he look at you before or after pressing? Does he perform a related action afterward—like going to the door after "outside"? Other cues, such as tail wags, whining, pacing, or persistent pressing, can provide additional evidence. Weekly notes on context, his responses, and your actions help reveal emerging patterns.

Accept some ambiguity. Sometimes a button gets stepped on by accident or pressed in excitement. In those moments, acknowledge the effort lightly and wait for a more intentional press before responding. If you're unsure, wait for another attempt or gently prompt—"Do you want to 'play'?" or the simpler "want 'play'?"—and watch his reaction.

As learning continues, boundary-testing is normal. Out-of-context words don't necessarily mean he's confused— he may be exploring how to use familiar words in new ways. Remember, the goal is not perfection. What matters are the steady, overall trends in consistency and clarity. Continue prompting correct use, praising appropriate presses, and keeping a log. Over time, you'll see the shift from random to purposeful conversation.

INTENT CHECKLIST: HOW TO KNOW WHEN HE REALLY MEANS IT

Use this checklist to help gauge intent and guide your responses:

☐ **Pressed the same button** three or more times in a consistent context

☐ **Made eye contact or showed focused posture** before or after pressing

☐ **Followed up with behavior** that matched the request (e.g., went to the door after "outside")

☐ **Showed emotional cues**—tail wag, whining, pacing

- ☐ **Persisted—repeated the press** when ignored
- ☐ **Received light acknowledgment** for ambiguous presses
- ☐ **Waited for a contextually relevant second press** when needed

Use this checklist to decode intent, support your dog's confidence, and strengthen your growing communication partnership.

Expanding Emotional Vocabulary—Teaching Feelings and Preferences

Once your dog is comfortable using communication buttons for basics, you can begin expanding into emotions and preferences—words like "happy," "mad," "no," and "love." These additions deepen your connection, allowing him to share inner experiences and make choices. A dog who presses "no" to refuse a treat or "mad" when a delivery person brings a package becomes more confident and empowered, avoiding misunderstandings and strengthening mutual trust.

Teaching these emotional and preference buttons requires patience, timing, and good observation. Start with clear, unmistakable moments. Press "happy" when he's obviously excited—after play, cuddles, or an enthusiastic greeting. Say the word, press the button, and respond with warm attention as he shows signs of joy (tail wag, wiggle, bright expression). For "no," notice moments when he truly refuses something—turning down a treat, backing away from brushing, or stepping back from a new object. Say "no," press the button, and gently remove or stop the activity. Use "no" only when refusal is apparent; otherwise, the concept becomes muddied.

Emotion words like "mad" can be taught through everyday frustrations, not fear. After learning the word "mad," Paddy was quick to use it in fitting situations. After barking ferociously at the door and setting off the other dogs, Paddy gave one more sharp "boof," then trotted to the board and pressed "mad." It wasn't stress or alarm—just a clear opinion about the disruption. On another day, I accidentally sat on his favorite blanket. Paddy stopped, stared, huffed once, and marched to the board to press "mad," returning to give me an unmistakable look. These moments show how dogs can use an emotion button to express simple frustrations in honest, appropriate ways.

Reinforcement strengthens emotional vocabulary by showing your dog that his words matter. If he presses "no" for a toy, say, "Okay, no toy now," and put it away. When he presses "mad," acknowledge it gently—"I see you're mad, Paddy. Paddy's mad."—and adjust the situation if it's appropriate to do so. If "happy" follows a walk, respond with affection or another joyful cue. Showing that his emotional presses matter teaches him that his feelings are recognized, fostering an honest, confident use of these words.

As his vocabulary grows, you can begin adding simple follow-up questions. Once he's using emotion words consistently, you can add "why" and try short prompts such as, "Why are you mad?" or model the sequence "why mad?" These questions aren't tests; they simply invite him to share more when he's ready. Some dogs ignore the prompt, others add a second word, and some respond later when they've processed it. The goal isn't perfect answers—it's opening the door for deeper communication.

Look for patterns rather than interpreting single presses too strongly. Communicating about feelings is deeply rewarding, but avoid overinterpreting a single press. Look for reliable patterns: Is "mad" used mostly when routines change? Is "no" used for certain foods or grooming tasks? Keep brief notes about the context, his behavior before and after pressing, and any patterns that emerge. If he presses "mad" during play yet seems relaxed and waggy, he may simply be experimenting with the word rather than expressing genuine irritation. As his real-world use expands, emotional words become more precise and more accurate.

Ethical teaching keeps emotional communication honest and safe. Never tease, provoke, or intentionally frustrate him to "test" an emotion button. Honor every press, even if it's inconvenient. If he presses "no" during grooming, pause and consider whether brushing might be uncomfortable or confusing. Responding with empathy keeps communication nurturing and trustworthy.

Reflecting on this progress highlights how far your dialogue has come. Enriching your dog's vocabulary with feelings and preferences builds a deeper partnership. You won't interpret every emotional word button press perfectly— and that's okay. What matters is your willingness to listen, respond gently, and respect his boundaries. These shared moments strengthen your connection in ways simple commands never could. As you finish this chapter, reflect on how far your dialogue has come—from basic needs to shared feelings. This progress marks a meaningful shift since the initial use of the buttons. Next, we'll explore how your dog may use language skills to solve problems, tell simple stories, and link experiences across time.

Chapter 11

Button Technology and Maintenance

Mild soap, warm water, canned air, and
towels are your button-cleaning toolkit.

Selecting communication buttons should feel a lot like choosing your dog's first leash—personal, practical, and based on what actually works for your dog. With so many brands and styles on the market, narrowing your choice to the features that matter most will save you time, frustration, and money. Below is a straightforward guide to what truly matters when selecting buttons, plus the brands most commonly used by experienced "talking dog" families.

Top Brands to Know
• Hunger for Words (Standard size)

Created by Christina Hunger, the speech-language pathologist whose work helped spark the entire "talking dog" movement. This brand is especially beginner-friendly because its buttons come with accessible training tools and step-by-step guides—some of which you'll see referenced throughout this book. While they don't publish exact pressure numbers, users say they're easy for dogs to press and simple for families to use. These buttons integrate smoothly into expanding boards and are intuitive for early learners.

• FluentPet (Compact size)

One of the most widely recognized names in dog-communication buttons and a favorite among experienced "talking dog" households. FluentPet's compact buttons require about 0.5 lbs of pressure, and their modular tile system is explicitly designed for vocabulary growth. Their mat layout expands as your dog learns new words—perfect for families who want to add new words every few weeks and build a true communication board over time. These buttons are consistent, durable, and built for long-term use.

• Kimpok (High-Sensitivity, Rechargeable Buttons)

A useful option for very small dogs, seniors, gentle-nosed dogs, or those with mobility limitations. Kimpok buttons require only ~0.2 lbs of pressure, making them one of the easiest-to-press options available. Their compact size and rechargeable design make them a good fit for dogs who struggle with standard-force buttons.

What Matters Most When Choosing Buttons

Durability

There's a big difference between novelty "toy buzzers" and buttons meant for real, daily use. All major brands use hard plastic shells, so what matters most is overall sturdiness: solid housing, tight seams, and a responsive press. Budget buttons may crack, pop apart, or slide across the floor; higher-quality brands tend to hold up better over time.

If sliding is a concern—especially on hardwood or tile—place the buttons on a silicone mat, or better yet, anchor your buttons in an interlocking tile system, which provides stability and helps organize your growing board.

Tactile Feedback

Some buttons "click" or offer slight resistance, letting your dog know they've triggered the button.

This can be helpful for:

- dogs with sensory or mobility challenges
- dogs who benefit from a clear tactile cue
- early learners building confidence with the button

Pressure

One of the most important—and most overlooked—features.

- Small dogs, seniors, or gentle nose-pressers do best with buttons requiring less than 0.5 lbs of force.
- Kimpok offers ultra-light presses (~0.2 lbs).
- FluentPet is light enough for most dogs.
- Hunger for Words doesn't publish press-force numbers but is widely described as beginner-friendly.

Size

A standard-size button is around 3½ inches wide—ideal for big dogs and paw pressers, but too large or stiff for many small dogs.

Compact buttons (typically under 2.5 inches) work better for small dogs, tiny paws, or mobility-limited dogs.

Profile (Height)

Most buttons share a similar height, but very flat "tablet-style" buttons are starting to appear. These look sleek but often lack traction, durability, and the modular layout needed for true vocabulary growth. They're best avoided unless you plan to keep your board limited to just a few words.

Sound Quality

Most of today's buttons use simple, low-quality speakers, so a clear recording makes a big difference. Record your words in a happy, upbeat voice—just as you usually speak to your dog—while holding the button 6–8 inches from your mouth. A clear, cheerful tone goes a long way toward making the playback recognizable. Re-record as needed to be sure your word is crisp, clear, and easy for your dog to understand.

Expandability

If you plan to teach more than a handful of words, choose a system built for growth.

Both Hunger for Words and FluentPet excel at providing:

- add-on buttons
- modular layouts
- organized boards that allow for expansion every 2–4 weeks

For beginners, starting with one to three buttons is plenty. Add new words slowly as your dog begins using their first buttons consistently.

As you embark on your button-training journey, consider purchasing a starter set—such as the FluentPet Starter Kit, which includes six buttons and three hexagonal mats, or the Hunger for Words Talking Pet Starter Set with four buttons and a button mat.

Ease of Recording

Choose buttons with simple, clearly labeled record and play controls. The easier it is to update the button, the smoother your training sessions will be—especially in a busy household where accidental erasing can happen.

Final Takeaway

Choose buttons your dog can press comfortably and that you can expand over time. Ignore flashy marketing and focus on the features that matter: pressure, size, sturdiness, and long-term layout support. The right buttons make learning smoother for everyone and set your dog up for meaningful communication success. Remember, no button system is perfect—what matters most is choosing one that your dog can press comfortably and confidently.

CHOOSING THE RIGHT BUTTON SYSTEM

Use this checklist to narrow your options before you buy.

☐ **What size** is my dog?

☐ **How strong** is her natural press?

☐ **Is she more likely** to press with her paw or her nose?

☐ **Does she have arthritis** or mobility challenges?

☐ **Do I plan to expand** beyond 4–8 words?

☐ **Do I prefer rechargeable** or battery-based buttons?

☐ **Will the buttons be used** indoors only?

☐ **Do I want training support** included?

Taking a moment to reflect on these questions will help you select a button system that fits both your dog's abilities and your long-term training goals.

Button Care and Maintenance—Cleaning, Batteries, and Lifespan

Proper button care keeps your dog's "voice" working reliably. A few simple habits prevent most problems.

Cleaning

Dogs use their paws and noses and come in from outside regularly, so buttons tend to collect dirt quickly.

Keep cleaning simple:

• Wipe surfaces every few days using a soft cloth and a pet-safe cleaning solution.

• After messy use, remove batteries and clean the shell with a damp, soapy cloth (never submerge).

• For sticky areas, use a cotton swab with diluted vinegar—keeping liquid away from the speaker.

• Lift mats weekly to clear dust, fur, or crumbs that may affect function.

Battery Care

Most buttons use AAA batteries, with some models (like Kimpok) using USB-rechargeable power.

• Use quality batteries to prevent leaks and rapid drain.

• Rechargeables should be topped up every 2–3 weeks or whenever sound weakens.

• Recycle batteries through local programs.

***Note:** Keep all batteries out of reach of children and pets, as swallowing or chewing them can be extremely dangerous.

Protecting Your Buttons

• Keep buttons dry and out of heat or direct sunlight.

• If you're not using an interlocking mat system, place buttons on silicone mats to prevent sliding.

• Encourage gentle presses from both dogs and people.

• For travel or storage, cushion buttons by wrapping them or placing them in a padded pouch or box.

• Alternatively, store buttons in a clear hanging organizer or in small craft boxes.

Troubleshooting

If a button stops working, try:

• Removing the batteries.

• Cleaning battery contacts.

• Using canned air to clear seams.

• Trying fresh batteries or fully recharging.

If issues persist, replacement is usually easier than repair—especially with budget models. Keep receipts if warranty support is available.

🐾 🐾

Routine Maintenance Checklist

Use this list to stay on top of simple habits that keep your dog's buttons working well.

- ☐ **Wipe surfaces every 2–3 days** if they're accumulating dirt
- ☐ **Deep-clean after outdoor** or messy use
- ☐ **Clear debris under mats** weekly
- ☐ **Replace or recharge batteries** when buttons show signs of battery fatigue, such as muffled sound or slow playback. (Depending on your dog's button use, monthly may be a good interval.)
- ☐ **Store and recycle batteries safely**
- ☐ **Keep buttons dry** and out of direct heat or sun
- ☐ **Encourage gentle presses**
- ☐ **Replace buttons that fail** after cleaning

Consistent care keeps your dog's communication clear, reliable, and frustration-free.

*Batteries are one of the most toxic materials** to enter landfills, highly dangerous to pets and wildlife, and among the most important items to recycle. For this reason—as well as their cost—it's best not to replace them prematurely. Instead of swapping every battery at once, consider replacing one-quarter, one-third, or half of your dog's button-board batteries at a time, on a schedule that fits your budget and your dog's level of use.

Troubleshooting Tech Glitches—Quick Fixes for Common Button Problems

Technology can be your best partner—when it works. Here are the most common issues you'll encounter and how to fix them quickly so your dog's communication isn't interrupted.

Silence is the most common problem. Check battery alignment or replace the batteries. After changing batteries, record a clear test word in a quiet room and test playback.

Stuck buttons often mean grit or hair inside. Lift the button from the board, gently tap or shake out any debris, and clear the seams with a tiny brush—such as a sewing machine cleaning brush, a small electronics brush, or an old-style camera air blower with a brush. Wipe surfaces with a damp cloth, avoiding moisture near electronics. If the button top has shifted out of place, gently tap, twist, or wiggle the button to help it settle back into position. If it remains jammed after cleaning, replace it.

Distorted sound usually results from background noise or muffled speech during recording. Record in a quiet area, six to eight inches from your mouth at a natural pace. If playback is unclear, erase and re-record. Persistent distortion may require new batteries or gentle cleaning around the microphone port.

Intermittent function—where a button works only sometimes—often points to low batteries, loose internal connections, or debris on the base. Replace batteries first. If problems continue, inspect mats and bases for residue, clean thoroughly, allow to dry, and test again. Issues that worsen with temperature or humidity may require moving the board to an area with more stable temperature and moisture levels.

Backup buttons are essential. Keep at least one spare

recordable button—ready to label—so you can swap it in immediately if a word fails. Place it in the same location on the board to maintain your dog's routine and prevent confusion.

When all else fails, check the manual or the manufacturer's troubleshooting guide. If your button is still under warranty, contact customer support with your purchase details and a brief summary of the steps you've already tried; this speeds up support. *(At this time, FluentPet offers a 2-year warranty on all its products, covering manufacturing defects.)*

Staying prepared—and addressing issues early—keeps communication smooth and frustration low for both you and your dog.

Creating a Button Bank—Storing and Labeling Future Words

A button bank is your set of "future words" ready to introduce as your dog learns. Training happens in spurts—today it's "yes" and "no", tomorrow it's words like "happy" and "mad". Having extra buttons prepared lets you capture those moments without delay.

Start with spare buttons. Keep at least two to four on hand, because the goal is to add two to four new words every two to four weeks or so. Buying a pack of four to six buttons is more cost-effective if you plan to add words steadily or train multiple pets.

Stay organized. It's easy to lose track of loose buttons—or, if you live with a retriever, have them happily carried off. Use a clear bin or box with snug dividers to keep dust away. Labeled pouches, small electronics organizers, or handmade foam-lined boxes all work well—especially for travel. Pack a couple of blank buttons and labels in your training bag so you're ready to introduce new words at any time.

Label clearly. Skip flimsy tape. Use waterproof labels or boldly printed, durable stickers. For handlers with vision limitations, add tactile markers such as raised dots, puffy paint, or Braille. Color coding helps too—blue for water, green for outdoor words, red for "no" or "all done". Label-writer labels are especially useful in kitchens and near water bowls—they're easy to read and tend to stay put.

Maintain an inventory. Track your button words so you stay aligned with your plan. Keep a list inside your storage bin or in your training log—along with label tape or stickers, writing markers, and any notes you want to remember. In multi-trainer households, hold brief check-ins to choose the next words together. Encourage the whole family to contribute —kids often notice cues adults miss.

Plan for space. Know how many open spots you have on your board or mat. If you're running low, add another mat or sketch a quick grid to map out future placement. Planning ahead helps prevent confusion as your dog begins combining more complex word groupings.

A button bank isn't just storage—it's a tool that fuels your dog's language growth. Organization prevents last-minute scrambling and helps everyone stay consistent with training. Each step in planning, storing, and labeling brings you closer to natural, effortless conversation with your dog. With an orderly button bank, you're fully prepared for the next step: helping your dog build complex phrases and enjoy deeper, more meaningful exchanges.

🐾 🐾

TRAINER'S TIP: PRE-RECORDED BUTTONS VS. RECORDING YOUR OWN

Pre-recorded buttons can be appealing—just press and go—but they come with limitations. Only one major brand currently offers them (Hunger for Words), and their word list is limited to a curated starter set. This can be helpful for beginners, since the words are chosen by button-training expert Christina Hunger, but it also means:

- You're limited to that brand's regular-size buttons
- You can't adjust tone, pace, pitch, or emotional warmth
- You may outgrow the included vocabulary quickly
- You lose the flexibility to record personalized words ("Grandma", "beach", "snuggle", "later", "help", toy names, etc.)

Recording your own words offers the most freedom. You choose the phrasing, tone, and emotional nuance—your dog hears your voice, spoken naturally in the way you already communicate with them. It also lets you expand vocabulary at your own pace, with words that match your dog's life, environment, and personality.

Bottom line: Pre-recorded buttons offer convenience, but recording your own gives you the customization, flexibility, and clarity your dog will rely on as their vocabulary grows.

Intermediate & Advanced Talkers—Building True Conversations

As your dog moves into the intermediate stage, expect more questions, more creative combinations of familiar words, and the occasional frustration as their desire for communication grows faster than their vocabulary. Keep modeling, responding, and introducing new words at 2–4-week intervals as long as they continue to seem ready and engaged.

Expect familiar words to take on new meanings as intermediate talkers often stretch the words they already know to describe a wide range of situations. "Water" might mean their bath, your child's bath, watering the garden, the sprinkler, the kiddie pool, the hydrotherapy pool, or the beach. Even short sequences like "all done," "go," "water" can shift meaning: we're done playing at the beach, you're finished watering the plants, Johnny's bath is over, your book-reading time needs to pause because their bowl is empty, they want to go swimming, or they definitely do not want a bath.

This flexible use of familiar words is normal. Give yourself time to interpret them in light of the situation and your knowledge of your dog—they may surprise you with how they're trying to use their language to talk to you.

INTERMEDIATE TALKER CHECKLIST—IS YOUR DOG READY FOR MORE WORDS?

Add new words when your dog is ready and the situation calls for them.

☐ **They regularly use most of the words** they already have.

☐ **They use some words** but avoid others.

☐ **They've started combining** words.

☐ **They seem frustrated** around the board.

☐ **There's a change in routine** or environment.

They may surprise you with just how creatively they use their expanding language.

Advanced Talkers—Intent, Sequencing, and Emotion

As dogs move into the advanced stage, their communication becomes more intentional and layered. They often self-correct, revisit a button when they feel misunderstood, and use longer sequences with surprising clarity. Advanced talkers draw on a vocabulary of 20 or more words and start expressing ideas in ways that show real thought.

Expect more complex combinations and more precise meaning. Advanced talkers may express time ("outside" "now" "Mommy"), needs ("Paddy" "want" "dental-chew"), and preferences ("play" "ball" "more"). You'll also begin to notice descriptive or relational words getting paired with action words—evidence that your dog is building simple grammar. Some dogs link past experiences to present emotions, such as Drake pressing "dog" "mad" "walk" after an overly-friendly dog rushed toward him on yesterday's walk. They may press words in a purposeful sequence or use a category button, like "toy," "outside," or "friend", before refining their message.

Expect emotional and social communication to expand. Words like "mad," "sad," "scared," "happy," "love," or "help" appear more frequently and with clearer context. Some dogs use emotional vocabulary to label their own feelings, while others use it to comment on yours or another animal's. Problem-solving vocabulary also increases—your dog begins combining words to explain what they want, what's wrong, or what needs to happen next.

Expect more intention, but also more nuance. Advanced talkers sometimes press an imprecise word not because they're confused, but because it's the closest option they have. This is flexible thinking, not error. Continue to model upgraded vocabulary so they can refine their meanings over time. When your dog strings together multiple words and waits for your response, they're not just pressing buttons— they're participating in a conversation.

Encourage your dog to build longer sentences through modeling and recasting. Recasting means repeating what your dog says and adding to it. As your dog becomes more accomplished with buttons, continue modeling and recasting every day. Narrate your interactions with him, just as you would with a toddler—he learns in much the same way. Repeat words back to him and ask what he wants. He says "Drake" "want". You say "What" "want", "Drake"? Then pause. Give him time. If he doesn't answer, say "Drake" "want" "chew bone" "yes"? Offer choices. Introduce simple yes or no questions. You will be amazed at what he is learning and what he has to say.

Introducing Advanced Concepts

Once your dog is confidently using their buttons—
pressing ten or more words independently, combining them throughout the day, and communicating across different situations—they may be ready for more advanced concepts. These ideas help your dog express emotions, experiences, and questions that go beyond simple requests.

Questions like who, what, where, and when allow your dog to take a more active part in communicating with you. Dogs ready for question words usually use buttons daily, combine words reliably, and frequently look for familiar people or objects. These early behaviors show they're already thinking in ways that questions can support.

Body part words such as eyes, ears, mouth, feet, tail, tummy, and back help your dog talk about their own body. This becomes incredibly useful for veterinary care, grooming, and comfort. If your dog has sensitivities, past injuries, or simply loves certain kinds of scratches, body-part words give them more control and a way to report discomfort. Including a word like ouch or hurt can empower them to tell you when something feels wrong.

Time concepts such as now, soon, later, tonight, and tomorrow introduce a sense of timing and anticipation. Dogs who are already combining words and referencing things from earlier in the day—or who clearly anticipate upcoming events —tend to pick up time concepts well. These words help them express expectations, preferences, and routines.

Emotion words like happy, sad, mad, scared, upset, and excited give your dog language for feelings they already show through body posture and expression. If you often find yourself trying to decode why they seem uneasy, excited, or disappointed, emotion words can help bridge that gap. When a dog regularly communicates and clearly displays emotions you understand through their body language, they're typically ready for this category.

Prepositions like on, off, up, down, in, and out introduce directional and spatial awareness—important building blocks for more complex communication later on. These concepts help your dog describe where things are or where they want to be, making their messages clearer and more actionable.

As your dog grows into these advanced concepts, their communication becomes richer, more nuanced, and surprisingly expressive. Introducing these ideas at the right time keeps learning fun, supports clarity, and strengthens your connection as your conversations evolve together.

Advanced Talker Checklist—Is Your Dog Ready For More Complex Concepts?

Understanding when your dog is ready for deeper ideas helps you introduce new words at the right time and pace.

☐ **They use at least ten words** on their own.
☐ **They combine words several times** a day.
☐ **They use words for reasons** other than requests.
☐ **They communicate with different people** in your home.
☐ **They use their buttons in a variety** of contexts or situations.

These signs show your dog is ready to explore richer concepts and broaden their communication.

Chapter 12

Tracking Progress, Building Community, and Lifelong Enrichment

Before you switch to a full logbook, even a simple magnetic chart can help you track your dog's growing vocabulary and celebrate each "Good Job"—especially helpful for young kids.

Mastering Progress Tracking—Logs and Milestones

The smallest moments can reveal the biggest progress.
Every day details during button training often mark the true
milestones in your dog's growth. Imagine sipping your
morning coffee and noticing your dog pressing "outside" on
her own. These subtle moments, easy to overlook amidst
routine, are vital—signaling connection and learning.

Your awareness should be tuned to her behavior. By
this time in your training, your "radar" should always be tuned
to your dog's behavior around the buttons, and you should be
listening for presses even if you're in another room. Take care
to notice a button that doesn't fully engage, too—sometimes
your dog will only partially press it, but the attempt still
deserves acknowledgment and encouragement. These near-
misses often show growing confidence or curiosity, and they
matter just as much as the clear, audible activations.

Logging becomes one of your most motivating tools.
At first, logging button usage might seem tedious, but it
quickly proves itself both helpful and motivating. A simple
note—"pressed 'water' at 7:30 a.m. after walk" or "used 'play'
after dinner"—forms a living record of communication
attempts. What you once celebrated as her very first press,
"eat," you may celebrate again in a whole new way when it
becomes her first three-word sentence: "Lilly" "want" "eat"!

Patterns in your log help shape the path ahead. As the
entries accumulate, they start to tell a compelling story—
revealing which words matter most to your dog and which go
unused. Context matters, too: Was she more vocal after guests
left? Did she use "water"—or even "want" "water"—more during
a heatwave? Details like these help guide effective

troubleshooting, inform thoughtful adjustments to your training plan, and reveal progress that might otherwise go unnoticed.

A dedicated logbook elevates the entire routine. Using a dedicated logbook enhances this routine in ways that soon feel indispensable. The Button Training for Dogs companion logbook provides structured daily and weekly entry spaces, places to note button presses, any pertinent details, and room to record observations or unexpected behaviors. It also includes space for milestones like "first pressing 'play,'" "combining two words," or "using 'scared' during a storm," along with thoughtfully designed progress checklists. These checklists keep you on track and help you see patterns at a glance—moments of growth, plateaus, and breakthroughs that can otherwise disappear in the blur of daily life. And as the months pass, many families find the logbook naturally becoming its own quiet treasure: a small keepsake of their dog's emerging voice and the journey they took together. Over time, these consolidated notes reveal trends that might go unnoticed day to day—and they invite the whole family to celebrate shared successes.

Recording first uses adds clarity and insight. Documenting the first use of each new word is especially powerful. Record the date, time, and situation—"pressed 'treat' after hearing the biscuit jar," or "first time she pressed 'Lilly' 'outside' after a walk"—and over time, you'll start to see patterns. Maybe she experiments with new words most in the afternoon, or presses "want" "cuddle" "now" before bed. Insights like these help you adjust button placement, timing, or reinforcement strategies. Noticing frequent "water" requests on hot days, for example, might prompt you to set out a cool outdoor water bowl or bring out the sprinkler or dog pool. These subtle but actionable patterns help you anticipate her needs with confidence and empathy.

Monthly reviews keep communication evolving. Set aside a few minutes to reflect: Which buttons are favorites? Are some rarely used? Do any seem to cause confusion? Use these reflections to make small, smart changes—retire irrelevant words, refresh neglected ones by pairing them with fun activities, or introduce new words tied to current interests. Maybe "snowball" made sense in winter, but not anymore; swap it for something she's excited about right now.

Personalized goals build confidence for both of you. Setting realistic, customized goals based on what you see in the log keeps the experience motivating. Instead of chasing viral-level breakthroughs, focus on achievable benchmarks: "Introduce two new words this month," or "Practice using 'help' in different situations this week." Each minor progression—bravely trying new words or refining familiar ones—builds confidence for both handler and dog and reduces frustration.

INTERACTIVE ELEMENT: PROGRESS TRACKING REFLECTION CHECKLIST

Weekly prompts to help you spot real communication growth.
☐ **List three discoveries** about your dog's communication (e.g., "uses 'Lilly' 'treat' after guests," "presses "nap" after lunch").
☐ **Identify her most and least used words.**
☐ **Write a goal** for the coming week ("I will say my emotions

out loud this week—e.g., I am 'mad,' or happy'—before adding those buttons").

☐ **Note a weekly highlight** (e.g., Lilly said 'no' when Sammy laid on her bed!).

Reflection helps you put the small pieces into a bigger picture. Taking a moment each week to reflect deepens understanding, reduces frustration, and helps you appreciate your overall progress better.

Sharing Success—Joining Support Groups and Online Communities

Button training can feel like crafting a new language with your dog — which it is!—and sharing these moments is exciting and rewarding. Support groups and online communities provide not just advice but also encouragement, reminding you and your dog that you're participating in a larger movement.

Facebook groups on button training, such as "Dog Button Training - Support & Sharing," are lively, welcoming spaces where members share videos, advice, and daily successes. Open to everyone—novices, seasoned trainers, even teens—these communities foster shared learning and camaraderie. Sharing your dog's "outside" breakthrough brings cheers, tips, and affirmation. If you encounter a snag—like a failed button or waning interest—posting for support yields a range of responses, from practical troubleshooting to simple encouragement. Discussions are grounded in evidence-based practices, with members often linking to reputable trainers and research. Moderators ensure a safe, constructive environment, making it comfortable to ask questions and share vulnerable moments.

Instagram, via hashtags like #DogButtonJourney, connects button trainers worldwide. Through thousands of posts, you see authentic training—dogs eager or perplexed, but always learning. Sharing images and stories helps encourage others and sparks new ideas, from helpful button-board layouts to fun and creative labels. Instagram's format encourages inspiration through sharing photos and joyful reactions captured on video.

Reddit's r/dogtraining button threads offer in-depth community learning. Forum posts provide space for storytelling, problem-solving, and debate. Here, users document step-by-step progress, share log entries, and weigh in on what works and what doesn't. Whether you're dealing with setbacks or multi-pet complications, expect thoughtful answers and ongoing discussion. Many users post follow-ups, allowing everyone to track their progress over time.

When you join such spaces, engage constructively. If you share a "first phrase" video, describe your process and the challenges you went through. If you seek help—whether with layout or button mashing—make your questions very clear and be sure to thank people who reply. Avoid criticizing or making assumptions about other handlers; patience and respect foster a positive, welcoming community. Empathize with others who have setbacks, and feel free to share your own struggles; vulnerability helps people bond and facilitates collective growth.

Great ideas often come from unexpected places: perhaps a "button scavenger hunt" game, or a virtual "Button

Graduation" party where families showcase skills and share stories. Some members post playlists and printable board templates, or organize themed events, all of which spark creativity and enrich the training process.

Discussions range from building adapted boards for dogs with mobility needs to troubleshooting stubborn buttons to safe ways for children to participate. The collective wisdom means no one has to start from scratch. If you're feeling frustrated or have hit a plateau, these communities can help reignite your motivation. Being part of such a supportive network makes button training more meaningful—celebrated at home and around the world, amongst those who understand the dedication and love involved.

Celebrating Milestones—Badges, Certificates, and Creative Rewards

Every achievement—small or large—enhances button training for both trainer and dog. That first deliberate press represents more than a learned skill; it shows that you've taught a meaningful concept and your dog has processed it, understood it, and intentionally used it in communication. That's an incredible milestone for both of you. Celebrating these moments matters. Even simple rituals boost morale and motivation. When your dog earns recognition for a new word or the family admires a "First Press" certificate on the refrigerator, the accomplishment stays fresh and meaningful.

A Milestone That Changed Everything — Paddy's First Real Answer

Sometimes a milestone doesn't look tidy or cinematic. Sometimes it looks like real life: three dogs, a sleep-deprived human, a husband blissfully unaware in the next room, and the entire morning derailed—first by one dog vomiting up part of a toy, then by an unexpected pile of "ahem" on the carpet. I'd been up until 1:30 a.m., and the day started with cleaning supplies, paw-wiping, "water" modeling in the kitchen, and getting meds and breakfasts sorted for our little pack of three dogs. And in that chaos, the bar shifts— you start counting "everyone alive" as a win.

After the chaos settled, it was decision time. In our house, some mornings mean choosing: go with Mommy to the office, or "Get-in-Bed" with Daddy. And for Paddy, Daddy's warm blanket nest is the closest thing he has to paradise. Jimmy is already dancing behind me— office with Mommy! Drake could go either way. Paddy? Always Daddy.

But for some reason—maybe because I was running on fumes, maybe because I needed a win—I decided to ask him directly. I whispered the words and pressed the buttons: "Get-in-Bed" with "Daddy"— "yes"? His first answer was "dental-chew," so after removing that, I whispered again, softly: "Get-in-Bed" with "Daddy" — "yes"?

He paused. Thought about it. You could almost see the gears turning. Then he looked at me, and leaned toward the yes button. His press was a little sloppy—his blanket was in the way—and the button didn't quite

147

activate, but the intention was unmistakable. I saw it. He knew I saw it. And *he knew I knew he knew.*

The second I said "Yes"? he lit up. His ears came forward, his whole body wiggled in that little anticipatory way he does, and he gave me this look— like he understood the whole conversation in one breath. Then he turned and headed straight down the hall toward the bedroom with quiet, confident purpose.

I took off after him. By the time I reached the doorway, he was already climbing the little dog stairs onto the bed, tail doing those joyful, full-body swoops that start somewhere up the spine and take the whole dog along for the ride. I caught up to him just as he settled on the bed, and we hugged and smooched and had our silent celebration because we both knew exactly what had just happened: he had *answered* me. Truly answered me.

Only after that moment settled between us—that perfect click of shared understanding—did he dive under the blankets into his favorite place in the universe: Daddy's warm, snuggly, everything-is-right blanket cave.

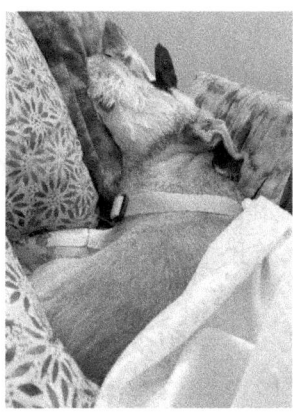

Paddy snuggled in bed between the pillows and blankets.

Recognition can be tangible or digital. Classic printable certificates—bright fonts, fun borders, and personal notes—invite pride, and kids can color them to add their own creative touch. Present a "Knows 5 Words" badge or sticker with playful ceremony, or display a wall of progress photos near your board. Each image captures a moment of growth—your dog beaming, you grinning, children laughing—reminding everyone of how far you've come.

For digital milestones, keep an online "Button Journey" album and post photos or videos to track progress. Many families design digital badges or build simple timelines to share with friends or on social media. Even a joyful group text can bring loved ones into the celebration.

Celebrations don't need to be elaborate. You might celebrate a new phrase your dog has mastered with a "toy day," surprising her with a new plaything that makes the moment feel special. Family "button cakes" give humans a treat while your dog enjoys her favorite snack or extra playtime. Some families throw a party—with hats, cupcakes, or a new button as a present—making each win feel special. Inventing your own traditions—like a silly dance, a homemade badge, or a painted rock for each new word— keeps training fun and enthusiasm alive, even during plateaus.

Including everyone enriches the celebration. Kids can add glitter and stickers to decorate badges and certificates, helping even modest achievements feel special. Grandparents may write congratulatory notes for the scrapbook. Teens might edit milestone videos or snap progress photos to share online. These moments, big or small, deepen the sense of shared achievement and make success communal.

Milestones deserve to be celebrated beyond home, too. Posting progress in support groups encourages others and sparks fresh celebration ideas. A collage or digital timeline can connect your family's journey to a larger audience, often inspiring new friendships.

Digital gatherings work just as well. Video calls with distant family give them a chance to see your dog's progress, admire the badge wall, or celebrate a new phrase. This allows friends and relatives to share in your accomplishments, keeping spirits high and highlighting your effort and growth. They invite your family to share in the joy of your progress from wherever they are.

Over time, these milestone moments become cherished memories. Looking back at badges, certificates, or photo strings, you'll remember not only what your dog achieved, but also the shared journey along the way. Such reminders also sustain momentum and help keep the spirit of learning alive.

Evolving Button Training—Adapting as Your Dog and Family Grow

Button training is inherently flexible; it evolves right alongside your household and your dog's life stage. No home stays the same—puppies grow up, seniors slow down, routines shift, and families expand. This adaptability keeps communication relevant and meaningful through all of life's changes.

New experiences often call for new vocabulary. If your once-calm dog becomes uneasy about car rides or visits to the vet, adding buttons like "vet" or "car ride" can help him anticipate what's coming and feel more secure. Words that no longer apply—like "beach" or "fetch" during quieter seasons—can be swapped out so the board continues to reflect your dog's actual world.

Welcoming a new family member, guest, or pet naturally expands your communication team. Start simple and positive: introduce friendly words for new arrivals ("hello," for example) to help your dog feel included. For young children, model simple, consistent button use and give them small jobs —like pressing "cuddle" at bedtime—to support their inclusion, bonding, and routine. When adding another dog, let each explore the board individually before practicing together so cues stay clear and individualized.

Reflecting on your growth as a trainer adds a valuable dimension to the journey. As you grow more confident in modeling, interpreting, recasting, and responding to your dog's communication, take time now and then to pause and reflect on how far you've come together. These reflections highlight the progress you've made not just as communicators, but as partners.

Think of button training as ongoing enrichment for you and your dog, not something with a finish line. Invite your household into simple challenges—like a "Learn a New Phrase Month"—so everyone has a chance to contribute and stay engaged. As your dog ages, consider adding comfort-focused buttons like "need help" or "soft bed," making sure his words remain useful and relevant as his needs change over time.

Stay open to experimentation. Life brings surprises—a move, a schedule shift, a health change—so treat these as opportunities to reinforce familiar words or introduce new ones. Keep the process lighthearted; mistakes and regressions are natural parts of an evolving learning experience.

Every adaptation—whether a new word, a new family member, or a new insight—enriches everyday life and brings your whole household closer. Each small step becomes part of your shared story, deepening understanding and connection as you go.

Let button training continue to grow with you and/or your family. Stay flexible, stay curious, and let each stage of life open the door to new ways of communicating with the dog you love. As you move forward, may the words you've built together spark joy, deepen your connection, and keep learning fresh, playful, and meaningful—no matter where life takes you.

CELEBRATION IDEAS FOR BUTTON TRAINING

Meaningful Ways to Celebrate Button Milestones
☐ **Print a certificate** for your dog's newest word or milestone

☐ **Create a digital badge** or simple progress tracker

☐ **Give a "milestone toy"** or extra-special chew or game

☐ **Have a family "button cake" night** (dog gets a safe treat, humans get dessert)

☐ **Build a milestone photo wall** or collage near the button board

☐ **Let kids design badges, stickers, or tiny awards**

☐ **Throw a small "button party"**—even simple hats and extra playtime count

☐ **Create an indoor "word garden" bowl** and add a decorated rock—painted, colored, or embellished with stickers or words—for each new word

☐ **Share a progress photo or video** with friends or your training community

☐ **Start a group text or video call** so loved ones can celebrate breakthroughs with you

Whether a milestone is big or small, celebrating it helps keep the journey joyful and meaningful.

Chapter 13
Conclusion

Paddy pressing his favorite "Yes" button.

Your Dog's Communication Journey Starts Here

You now have all the tools you need to teach your dog how to "talk"—not perfectly, not instantly, but in small, meaningful moments that build real understanding over time. Every new word is an act of trust. Every modeled press is an invitation. And every button on the board is another opportunity for your dog to express something true and important to them.

There will be days when your dog walks to the board with purpose and tells you exactly what they need. And there will be chaotic days, when enthusiasm takes over, and the buttons fly faster than the meaning. All of it counts. All of it is communication. Celebrate curiosity, intention, effort, and experimentation—these are the building blocks of real learning.

Sometimes, the most insightful moments happen when you least expect them. In our family, we used to call these "echo moments"—times when a child repeats something they've heard without fully absorbing it, just sounding it out. So when Paddy presses a word unexpectedly, I sometimes wonder: Is he expressing something fundamental here? Or simply echoing what he's heard? Is he responding to the emotion in the room, or sharing a thought of his own?

One evening, Karl came in from the rain after coaxing Drake to hurry up outside. Drake had been doing dog things—following a rabbit trail instead of the task at hand

—and Karl muttered a frustrated "Darn it, Drake" as he shut the door. A minute later, Paddy walked into my office, looked right at me, and pressed "no."

And again I wondered: Was it imitation, interpretation, or commentary? Was he letting me know that Daddy was annoyed because of Drake, or even tattling that Drake had been a little naughty?

I didn't know in that moment which it was—echo, commentary, or interpretation. But here's what I've learned since: Paddy is watching, and he is thinking. And now he knows I know. That mutual recognition—that sense of I see you seeing me—is real, and it's where the magic happens. We're all learning from each other, word by word, moment by moment. And it's happening because we finally share a way to talk about the world together.

Stay observant. Stay consistent. Stay flexible as your dog discovers the power of their new voice. You're not just teaching your dog to press buttons. You're creating a shared language—one you'll keep developing together, press by press, conversation by conversation.

Keep listening. Keep learning. And enjoy every conversation ahead.

Here's to many more words, many more moments, and a lifetime of conversations with your dog.

Enjoying your button-training journey?

If this book has helped you understand your dog, build stronger communication, or celebrate new moments of connection, I'd be grateful if you shared your experience with others.

Your review makes a meaningful difference.

A great review helps other dog lovers discover this book, supports indie authors, and encourages more people to begin their own communication journeys with their pets. Even a short review—just a few words—helps immensely.

Just scan the QR code below or click the link to go directly to this book's Amazon review page.

https://www.amazon.com/review/create-review?&asin=1971218022

Thank you for reading, learning, and listening to your dog.

Wishing you and your canine communicator many joyful conversations ahead.

— Karen E. Mueller, DVM

(also Drake, Paddy, and Jimmy)

With thanks from Drake, Paddy, and Jimmy.

Bonus Resources

Bonus Resources

To support your button-training journey, optional materials are available online, including printable badges, certificates, and other family-friendly tools designed to make learning engaging and fun.

Visit **KMuellerPublishing.com** to explore current resources and updates.

Recommended Resources

These books and studies offer deeper insight into how dogs think, learn, and communicate—laying the groundwork for understanding button-based communication. Each entry includes a short overview to help you understand why it matters and how it connects to your dog's learning journey.

Scientific Foundations of Canine Communication
Social learning and modeling (why dogs learn from what we show them)
Dogs learn powerfully by watching and imitating humans—an essential foundation for modeling button presses.
Fugazza, C., & Miklósi, Á. (2015). Social learning in dogs: A review. *Biology Reviews, 90*(4), 1237–1254. https://doi.org/10.1111/brv.12156
This review underscores why modeling your dog's buttons is such an effective teaching strategy.

How dogs use signals, gestures, and context to communicate

Understanding nonverbal communication helps you interpret your dog's button presses more accurately.

Hecht, J., Marshall-Pescini, S., & Range, F. (2022). What does the dog say? A review of research on canine vocal and nonvocal communication. *Animal Cognition, 25*, 1083–1101. https://doi.org/10.1007/s10071-022-01679-6

This work reminds us that button presses are just one part of a much broader communication system your dog already uses.

How dogs learn words—and sometimes overextend them

The famous "Rico" study shows that dogs can rapidly associate new labels with objects, even if early uses are broad or imprecise.

Kaminski, J., Call, J., & Fischer, J. (2004). Word learning in a domestic dog: Evidence for fast mapping. *Science, 304*(5677), 1682–1683. https://doi.org/10.1126/science.1097859

This foundational study supports the idea that early button use may be flexible before becoming more precise.

Building large vocabularies and understanding categories

The "Chaser" study demonstrates how dogs categorize words and meanings over time—similar to expanding a button board.

Pilley, J. W., & Reid, A. K. (2011). Border collie comprehends object names as verbal referents. *Behavioural Processes, 86*(2), 184–195. https://doi.org/10.1016/j.beproc.2010.11.007

This work illustrates how vocabulary can grow with consistent modeling and clear associations.

How animals learn symbols and structured communication systems

Symbol-based communication research helps explain why dogs can learn to use AAC buttons as meaningful markers.

Hopkins, W. D., & Washburn, D. A. (2020). Nonhuman animals' use of symbols: A comparative review. *Learning & Behavior, 48*(3), 215–229. https://doi.org/10.3758/s13420-020-00420-8

This review provides a scientific backdrop for understanding button presses as symbolic communication.

Canine Learning & Cognition
How dogs think, learn, and interpret human cues

This book offers broad scientific insight into dog behavior, cognition, and communication.

Miklósi, Á. (2014). *Dog behaviour, evolution, and cognition* (2nd ed.). Oxford University Press.

A strong resource for anyone wanting a deeper understanding of why dogs learn and communicate the way they do.

The social behavior behind our bond with dogs

This review explores why dogs attend closely to human behavior and why they are so attuned to our actions and signals.

Udell, M. A. R., & Wynne, C. D. L. (2011). The nature of dogs' social behavior: A review. *Animal Behaviour, 81*, 715–726.

This work reinforces the idea that communication is a partnership shaped by social connection.

Human–Dog Communication
Understanding your dog's social intelligence
This book provides an accessible look at how dogs read us—and how we read them.
Hare, B., & Woods, V. (2013). *The genius of dogs.* Penguin.
A great introduction to the incredible social and communicative skills dogs bring to button training.

A comprehensive academic overview of dog behavior and cognition
An essential read for anyone interested in the science behind dog–human relationships.
Serpell, J. (Ed.). (2016). *The domestic dog: Its evolution, behavior and interactions with people* (2nd ed.). Cambridge University Press.
This text offers context for understanding communication across training, evolution, and behavior.

Button-Based Communication (Practical Resources)
Introduction to AAC for dogs by a speech-language pathologist
Christina Hunger's work sparked the modern button-training movement.
Hunger for Words. (n.d.). Teaching dogs to "talk" using augmentative and alternative communication (AAC). https://www.hungerforwords.com
A practical starting point for understanding the origins of canine AAC training.

Guides, updates, and educational materials from a major button manufacturer

FluentPet provides structured layouts, research updates, and button-training strategies.

FluentPet. (n.d.). Educational resources for canine communication. https://fluent.pet

A useful resource for building consistent soundboard setups at home.

Conclusion

These resources support the science, practice, and philosophy behind button training. Whether you want to explore how dogs learn words, deepen your understanding of their communication skills, or simply strengthen your bond, each of these works can enrich your journey.

References

1. American Kennel Club. (n.d.). *Fun, cognitive training games to make your dog smarter.* https://www.akc.org/expert-advice/training/fun-cognitive-training-games-for-dogs/.

2. American Kennel Club. (n.d.). *How to bring your dog back into training after a break.* https://www.akc.org/expert-advice/training/how-to-bring-your-dog-back-into-training/.

3. American Kennel Club. (n.d.). *How to teach your dog to "talk" using buttons.* https://www.akc.org/expert-advice/training/how-to-teach-your-dog-to-talk/.

4. American Kennel Club Pet Insurance. (n.d.). *Dog fatigue: When to end a training session.* https://www.akcpetinsurance.com/blog/canine-fatigue-6-signs-your-training-session-is-done-/.

5. Bailey, I., & Myers, L. (2010). Border collie comprehends object names as verbal referents. *Behavioural Processes, 86*(2), 184–195. https://doi.org/10.1016/j.beproc.2010.11.007.

6. Business Insider. (2025). *The 4 best dog talking buttons in 2025.* https://www.businessinsider.com/guides/pets/best-dog-buttons/.

7. What About Bunny. (n.d.). What About Bunny YouTube channel. https://www.youtube.com/channel/UCEa46rlHqEP6ClWitFd2QOQ/.

8. FluentPet. (n.d.). *The complete guide to teaching dogs to talk with buttons.* https://fluent.pet/pages/getting-started-with-talking-buttons/.

9. FluentPet. (n.d.). *Planning your soundboard.* https://fluent.pet/blogs/learning-center/planning-your-soundboard/.

10. FluentPet Community. (n.d.). *My learner won't press the buttons.* https://community.fluent.pet/c/button-teaching-faqs/1-my-learner-won-t-press-the-buttons-won-t-press-them-unprompted/.

11. FluentPet Community. (n.d.). *Starting buttons with "older" dogs.* https://community.fluent.pet/c/discussion/starting-buttons-with-older-dogs/.

12. FluentPet Community. (n.d.). *Wall mounted soundboard for disabled dog.* https://community.fluent.pet/c/discussion/wall-mounted-sound-board-for-disabled-dog/.

13. Fugazza, C., & Miklósi, Á. (2015). Social learning in dogs: A review. *Biological Reviews, 90*(4), 1237–1254. https://doi.org/10.1111/brv.12156.

14. Hare, B., & Woods, V. (2013). *The genius of dogs.* Penguin.

15. Happy With Dogs. (n.d.). *The power of consistency: How to get your entire*

References

family involved in dog training. https://happywithdogs.com/the-power-of-consistency-how-to-get-your-entire-family-involved-in-dog-training/.

16. Hecht, J., Marshall-Pescini, S., & Range, F. (2022). What does the dog say? A review of research on canine vocal and nonvocal communication. *Animal Cognition, 25*, 1083–1101. https://doi.org/10.1007/s10071-022-01679-6.

17. Highland Veterinary. (n.d.). *The power of breed-specific dog training.* https://highlandveterinary.com/the-power-of-breed-specific-dog-training/.

18. Hopkins, W. D., & Washburn, D. A. (2020). Nonhuman animals' use of symbols: A comparative review. *Learning & Behavior, 48*(3), 215–229. https://doi.org/10.3758/s13420-020-00420-8.

19. Hunger for Words. (n.d.). *Meet Stella, the world's first talking dog!* https://www.hungerforwords.com/.

20. Hunger for Words. (n.d.). *Resources: Dog button training tips.* https://www.hungerforwords.com/resources/.

21. Hunger for Words. (n.d.). *What is AAC?* https://www.hungerforwords.com/what-is-aac/.

22. Hunger for Words. (n.d.). *Why every dog owner should try button training.* https://www.hungerforwords.com/why-every-dog-owner-should-try-button-training/.

23. iPuppee. (n.d.). *Dog button communication: Guide for owners and trainers.* https://ipuppee.com/blogs/news/dog-button-communication-guide-owners-trainers/.

24. iPuppee. (n.d.). *Teaching dogs buttons: Simple guide for success.* https://ipuppee.com/blogs/news/teaching-dogs-buttons-guide/.

25. Kaminski, J., Call, J., & Fischer, J. (2004). Word learning in a domestic dog: Evidence for fast mapping. *Science, 304*(5677), 1682–1683. https://doi.org/10.1126/science.1097859.

26. Miklósi, Á. (2014). *Dog behaviour, evolution, and cognition* (2nd ed.). Oxford University Press.

27. Modern Dog Magazine. (n.d.). *Yes, you should "baby talk" to your dog.* https://moderndogmagazine.com/articles/yes-you-should-baby-talk-to-your-dog/.

28. Morningside Veterinary. (n.d.). *Teaching your pet to use talking paw buttons.* https://morningsideveterinary.com/teaching-your-pet-to-use-talking-paw-buttons/.

29. Pet Health Harbour. (2024, June 11). *A guide to caring for your senior dog.* https://pethealthharbour.com/aging/a-guide-to-caring-for-your-senior-dog/.

30. Pet Health Harbour. (2024, June 11). *How and what dogs see.* https://pethealthharbour.com/eyes/how-and-what-dogs-see/.

31. Pet Health Harbour. (2024, September 17). *Back-to-school blues: Helping your pet adjust to the routine.* https://pethealthharbour.com/blog-details/2024/09/17/back-to-school-blues-helping-your-pet-adjust-to-the-routine/.

32. Pet Health Harbour. (2024, October 1). *Strategies to reduce stress for pets at the vet clinic.* https://pethealthharbour.com/blog-details/2024/10/01/strategaries-to-reduce-stress-for-pets-at-the-vet-clinic/.

33. Pet Health Harbour. (2024, October 8). *Fall fitness: Adjust your dog's exercise for cooler weather.* https://pethealthharbour.com/blog-details/2024/10/08/fall-fitness-adjust-your-dogs-exercise-for-cooler-weather/.

34. Pet Health Harbour. (2024, November 19). *New place, no problem: Tips for a low-stress move for pets.* https://pethealthharbour.com/blog-details/2024/11/19/new-place-no-problem-tips-for-a-low-stress-move-for-pets/.

35. Pet Health Harbour. (2025, January 1). *New year, new habits: Kickstart your pet's health in January.* https://pethealthharbour.com/blog-details/2025/01/01/new-year-new-habits-kickstart-your-pets-health-in-january/.

36. Pet Health Harbour. (2025, January 30). *Dogs and what to know after your baby arrives: Part 3.* https://pethealthharbour.com/others/dogs-and-what-to-know-after-your-baby-arrives-part-3/.

37. Pet Health Harbour. (2025, May 5). *What your pet's body language is trying to tell you.* https://pethealthharbour.com/news/2025/05/05/what-your-pets-body-language-is-trying-to-tell-you/.

38. Pet Health Harbour. (2025, May 23). *How to spot hidden health issues in pets before they become serious.* https://pethealthharbour.com/blog-details/2025/05/23/how-to-spot-hidden-health-issues-in-pets-before-they-become-serious/.

39. Pilley, J. W., & Reid, A. K. (2011). Border collie comprehends object names as verbal referents. *Behavioural Processes, 86*(2), 184–195. https://doi.org/10.1016/j.beproc.2010.11.007.

40. Psych Dog Partners. (n.d.). *Training log downloads.* https://www.psychdogpartners.org/resources/getting-a-dog/training-logs/training-log-downloads/.

41. Reddit. (n.d.). *What to do about button mashing with a new learner.* https://www.reddit.com/r/PetsWithButtons/comments/132hwc8/what_to_do_about_button_mashing_with_a_new_learner/.

42. Resolve / Cambridge University Press. (n.d.). *When dogs talk: Technologically mediated human–dog interactions as semiotic assemblages.* https://resolve.cambridge.org/core/journals/signs-and-society/article/when-dogs-talk-technologically-mediated-humandog-interactions-as-semiotic-assemblages/D2D236B8311EC6ACD75557758415307E/.

References

43. The Spruce Pets. (2025). *The 7 best dog talking buttons of 2025.* https://www.thesprucepets.com/best-dog-talking-buttons-6455644/.

44. United States National Library of Medicine. (2023). Therapy and prevention of noise fears in dogs. *Frontiers in Veterinary Science, 10,* Article 976503. https://pmc.ncbi.nlm.nih.gov/articles/PMC10705068/.

45. Very Important Paws. (n.d.). *How to adapt training techniques as your dog ages.* https://www.veryimportantpaws.com/training-your-dog-life-adapting-techniques-ages/.

46. Whole Dog Journal. (n.d.). *Talking buttons for dogs.* https://www.whole-dog-journal.com/lifestyle/talking-buttons-for-dogs/.

Acknowledgments

This book exists because of the dogs who share our lives and continually remind us how much they are already communicating—if we're willing to slow down and listen. I'm deeply grateful to the families, clients, and readers who have trusted me with their dogs, their questions, and their learning curves. Your patience, curiosity, and willingness to try something new have shaped this work more than you know.

I owe special thanks to my own dogs, who have been my teachers in the truest sense—patient, opinionated, honest, and endlessly instructive. They have reminded me that communication is not about perfection, but about relationships.

I am also thankful to the broader community of trainers, educators, and advocates who continue to expand our understanding of how animals learn, express preferences, and participate actively in their own lives. Progress in this field happens because many people are thinking, questioning, and sharing generously.

In that spirit, I extend my thanks to Christine Hunger for her work applying AAC concepts to canine communication, for fostering curiosity and compassion about how dogs express themselves, and for developing the button tools and materials referenced in this book.

Finally, thank you to the readers holding this book. Whether you are working alone or as part of a family team, your willingness to approach communication with patience, kindness, and respect is what ultimately makes this work meaningful—for dogs and humans alike.

About the Author

Karen E. Mueller, DVM, is a veterinarian, educator, and author with a lifelong interest in how dogs learn and communicate. Her experience with dogs spans early work in 4-H, obedience training, and the breed ring, along with hands-on involvement in agility, nose work, and service dog training. Over the years, she has also supported clients and their dogs across a wide range of dog sports—including carting, dock diving, FAST CAT, tracking, and agility—giving her a broad, practical understanding of canine behavior, motivation, and partnership.

Through her veterinary background and daily life with her own dogs, Dr. Mueller brings a science-based, positive-reinforcement approach to button training—one that emphasizes clarity, consent, and emotional well-being. She blends animal health, education, and real-world experience to help families build thoughtful, respectful relationships with their dogs.

Also by Karen E. Mueller, DVM

Animal Communication & Behavior—Teach Them to Talk™ Series

Button Training for Dogs: Teach Your Dog to Talk — A Practical Guide to Button Communication

Dog Button Training Logbook: Track Your Dog's Words, Progress, and Milestones — A Companion Journal to Button Training for Dogs

Humor & Parenting—Some Things Suck™ Series

Some Moms Suck Way More Than You: 24 Animal Parenting Fails That Prove You're NOT a Bad Mom

Some Dads Suck Way More Than You: 22 Wild Examples That Prove Why You're a Great Dad

Coming Soon

Some Teens Suck Way More Than You: 20 Wild Examples That Prove You're Doing Better Than You Think

Some Babies Suck Way More Than Yours: 20 Wild Examples of Why Your Baby's the Best

Cryptozoology & Natural History—Creatures of the World™ Series

Cryptid Creatures of the World: An Illustrated Guide to Myths, Monsters, and Mysterious Creatures Haunting Six Continents

Criaturas Críptidas del Mundo: Una Guía Ilustrada de Mitos, Monstruos y Criaturas Misteriosas que Habitan en los Seis Continentes

Cryptids of the World: Where Legends Meet Reality

Críptidos del Mundo, Donde las Leyendas se Encuentran con la Realidad

Sasquatch: Insights into Their Lives and Encounters with Humans

www.ingramcontent.com/pod-product-compliance
Lightning Source LLC
Chambersburg PA
CBHW060139150626
46550CB00015B/1969